TRUE NORTH GROUPS

TRUE NORTH GROUPS

A Powerful Path to Personal and Leadership Development

Bill George and Doug Baker

BK

Berrett–Koehler Publishers, Inc.
San Francisco
a BK Business book

Berrett-Koehler Publishers, Inc.

235 Montgomery Street, Suite 650, San Francisco, CA 94104-2916

Tel: (415) 288-0260 • Fax: (415) 362-2512 • www.bkconnection.com

ORDERING INFORMATION

QUANTITY SALES. Special discounts are available on quantity purchases by corporations, associations, and others. For details, contact the "Special Sales Department" at the Berrett-Koehler address above.

INDIVIDUAL SALES. Berrett-Koehler publications are available through most bookstores. They can also be ordered directly from Berrett-Koehler: Tel: (800) 929-2929; Fax: (802) 864-7626; www.bkconnection.com

ORDERS FOR COLLEGE TEXTBOOK/COURSE ADOPTION USE. Please contact Berrett-Koehler: Tel: (800) 929-2929; Fax: (802) 864-7626.

ORDERS BY U.S. TRADE BOOKSTORES AND WHOLESALERS. Please contact Ingram Publisher Services, Tel: (800) 509-4887; Fax: (800) 838-1149; E-mail: customer.service@ingrampublisherservices.com; or visit www.ingrampublisherservices.com/Ordering for details about electronic ordering.

Berrett-Koehler and the BK logo are registered trademarks of Berrett-Koehler Publishers, Inc.

Printed in the United States of America

Berrett-Koehler books are printed on long-lasting acid-free paper. When it is available, we choose paper that has been manufactured by environmentally responsible processes. These may include using trees grown in sustainable forests, incorporating recycled paper, minimizing chlorine in bleaching, or recycling the energy produced at the paper mill.

LIBRARY OF CONGRESS CATALOGING-IN-PUBLICATION DATA

George, Bill (William W.)

True north groups: a powerful path to personal and leadership development / Bill George and Doug Baker. — 1st ed.

  p. cm.

Includes bibliographical references and index.

ISBN 978-1-60994-007-2 (pbk. : alk. paper)

1. Small groups. 2. Leadership. I. Baker, Doug, 1935– II. Title.

HM736.G46 2011

158´.4 — dc23

2011022891

First Edition

16 15 14 13 12 11   10 9 8 7 6 5 4 3

Project management and design by Valerie Brewster, Scribe Typography.

Copyediting by Todd Manza. Proofreading by Don Roberts. Index by George Draffan.

Cover image: istock © Stephen Strathdee.

*This book is dedicated to the members of our men's group
and our couples group who have shared with us
so much of themselves, their wisdom, their caring,
and their love for so many years.*

CONTENTS

MANY, MANY BOOKS COME ACROSS MY READING TABLE each year, but it has been a long time since one of them impressed me so much as this one has. It is a wisdom guide to help us to look deeper, to honor the essential and sacred traditions of living communities, and to take this "one wild and precious life" seriously.[1]

We are storytelling animals. As our hunter-gatherer ancestors sat around the fire carving arrows and eating berries, they told stories which in time were woven into the tapestry of daily life. These stories were the first encyclopedia of human knowledge. They explained where the world came from, why there are people, and why the gods put fire and death on earth. Stories told the people of a tribe who they were, where they had been, where they were going, and how to stay friendly with the spirits.

For over thirty years I have explored, researched, written about, and been invited to speak about how we shape our stories into more purposeful lives. Lately, more people have been asking if and how I am shaping my own story and what helps me sustain a purposeful journey day by day throughout the year.

I always find myself realizing that I could never live purposefully without my "tribe"—people who are on a shared path with me. By tribe, I mean people who truly "get me" and understand and reflect back to me my true story. They know how to pose a powerful question and are rarely reluctant to ask it. It is their curiosity that keeps me curious and alive.

To be a person is to have a story to tell. We become grounded in the present when we color in the outlines of the past and the future. Within each of us there is a tribe with a

complete cycle of stories. It is impossible to create a meaningful life alone. In truth, we do little completely alone. We
depend on a living community—a true north group—to
accompany us each step of the way. We might see ourselves
as self-sufficient, which I often do, but we ignore the essential, life-giving companionship upon which our very lives,
livelihoods, and longevity depend.

Bill and Doug clearly show us how to create that living community. They ask us wise questions and show us the
practices that lead us to our own answers. There is one question in particular that I find very compelling in my work as
an executive coach: "What are you *up to*?" Bill and Doug
believe, as I do, that each of us is up to something very special with our lives. They believe that each of us is born with a
unique gift and a sacred duty to fulfill its promise.

This gift, for each of us, is the pathway to a meaningful life. It is the pathway to our livelihood—our life's work.
All of life is viewed as a quest to answer the core true north
question, "What are you up to?"

Many of us at various points in our own lives are a little
vague about what we're up to. Maybe even utterly confused.

Poet Mary Oliver poses the question in another way:
"Tell me, what is it you plan to do with your one wild and
precious life?" Wild and precious? Do you reflect, as I do,
that you may not be living up to your precious possibilities
in life?

Doug and Bill have been living with this and similar
questions for many years! Perhaps this is why they created
their own True North Group over thirty years ago.

But this book is not about Doug and Bill; it's about you.
So, can we dig a little deeper? What is a "wild and precious
life" to you? And how does it differ from your current life?

Let's face it: just getting through life today with some
semblance of success is a major feat. Many of us, however,

spend less than 20 percent of our precious time engaged in what might be called meaningful activity—talking with friends about what matters, observing spiritual practices, helping others, or performing meaningful work. It doesn't have to be that way. Our precious lives don't have to be dominated by busyness.

We may find ourselves on different paths, but it's essential that we are on different paths together. Isolation is fatal! It's important that we don't tackle life alone. The gift is free. But its expression requires support. And that's the essence of a True North Group—to share the path in helping us claim our gift and heed our calling.

Still, it takes no small courage to be willing to seek company on our journey—to ask to be accompanied. For many years I belonged to a circle of a dozen men who called themselves the Junto. Patterned after Benjamin Franklin's group of the same name, we met nine times a year to exchange stories from our journeys and to share our challenges and blessings.

The magic of the Junto was due to the simple discovery that everyone yearned to share his story. When we tell our stories to one another, we—at one and the same time—find the meaning of our lives and are healed from our isolation and loneliness. Many religious traditions honor this essential practice. Likewise, many indigenous peoples honor this practice, realizing that they cannot possibly do the work of living, surviving, and healing alone.

We can't truly tell who we are unless someone is listening. Strange as it may seem, self-knowledge begins with self-revelation. We don't know who we are until we hear ourselves speaking the story of our lives to someone we trust to listen with an open mind and heart.

In my coaching work, I have rarely encountered a person who was not able to uncover the power of their individual purpose in a True North–type group and, having made that discovery, to find the possibility of truly living *up to* their wild and precious possibilities. Bill and Doug have made an important contribution indeed to that discovery process.

Richard Leider
Best-selling author of *The Power of Purpose* and
Repacking Your Bags

SINCE 1975, WE HAVE BEEN ACTIVELY INVOLVED IN small, personal groups that serve as the inspiration and the basis for True North Groups. True North Groups comprise six to eight peers who meet on a regular basis to discuss the important questions of their lives and to support each other during difficult times.

These groups have been a godsend in our lives and in the lives of hundreds of people we know. They have helped us navigate personal challenges with our families, our careers, and our health. They have provided a forum for addressing life's most difficult questions about our beliefs, our values, and the meaning and purpose of our lives.

Over the years we have frequently been asked by friends and acquaintances, "How can I form such a group?" Originally, we set out to write a book to answer that question, a "how to" manual for creating True North Groups, as both of us do in our work these days.

As we interviewed a wide range of people participating in groups and studied the small-group movement in its larger sociological context, however, we recognized there is a much greater need for these groups and that they are part of a broader societal shift toward forming small groups. Thus, we expanded our focus to looking at the essential role True North Groups can play in human growth and leadership development and in filling the void that many of us feel in our lives.

We believe there is a unique role for personal, intimate groups that differs from the multitude of groups formed for specific purposes. By providing a safe place for deep, intimate discussions about life's most challenging questions, True

North Groups enable us to become fully human and more fully alive, awakening to the enormous possibilities within each of us. They are the best vehicle we know for helping us develop as human beings and as leaders. In a world where the difficulties we face every day often feel overwhelming, True North Groups provide a powerful path between our personal lives and the organizations we participate in.

This book is written for you, if you are interested in forming such a group. Or perhaps you want to enable your current group to have deeper and more meaningful discussions about the vital questions of life. It offers you a deeper understanding of the vital role a True North Group can play in your life and how you can form one. It shows how to create sound norms that enable the group to navigate successfully through the inevitable storms that all groups encounter and to emerge as a high-performing group.

It is our hope that your experiences with your groups will be as meaningful and rewarding as ours have been.

Bill George and Doug Baker
Minneapolis, Minnesota
April 2011

Finding Depth and Intimacy in Your Life

WE YEARN TO SHARE THE STORIES OF OUR LIVES AND to have honest conversations with people we trust. Have you ever felt alone in a crowd? Were you eager to abandon the superficial conversations and share your authentic self and your feelings without fear of being judged?

We need people around us to whom we can look for support and advice, who can help us develop as human beings. We need them to help us become better leaders in our work, our communities, and our families. We want to be open and vulnerable, but who can we rely on to have our best interests at heart and maintain our confidentiality? Where can we find this kind of depth, intimacy, and support in our lives? Who do we talk to when we have great joy or sorrow in our lives or are facing difficult decisions?

The challenges we face these days are so great that we cannot rely entirely on ourselves, our communities, or our organizations to support us and help us stay on track. We need a small group of people with whom we can have in-depth discussions and share intimately about the most important things in our lives—our happiness and sadness, our hopes and fears, our beliefs and convictions.

We call these groups True North Groups because they help us follow our True North. As Bill wrote in his book by that name, True North represents what is most important to us in life: our beliefs, our most cherished values, our passions and motivations, and the sources of satisfaction in our lives. True North is the orienting point that keeps us on track as human beings and as leaders. It represents who we are at our deepest level.

Most of us know what our True North is, but we are constantly pressured by external forces to deviate from it. Or we are seduced by extrinsic rewards like money, power, and recognition that cause us to detour from our True North.

We created True North Groups to address our need for a support team to enable us to get through challenging times and to be there for us in good times and bad. By bridging the gap between our individual lives and the organizations and communities we engage every day, True North Groups can help us find joy and fulfillment in our lives. They can help us develop as authentic leaders who can make a difference in our world.

Before digging into what a True North Group is and why you would want to join one, we would like to share our stories of how we got interested in small groups.

BILL'S STORY

All my life I have been passionate about leadership. From observing leaders at a young age to leading business organizations and working with leaders committed to making a difference, I've always wanted to be engaged with leaders and with leading.

In my early years, I was never asked to lead anything, as I was too eager to get ahead. In high school and college, I was devastated as I lost seven consecutive elections, until some older friends helped me get on track. After that, I had many opportunities to lead organizations in college and graduate school before plunging into the world of business. There I spent ten years each at Litton Industries, launching the consumer microwave oven business, and at Honeywell, in a variety of executive leadership roles. It wasn't until 1989 that I arrived at Medtronic's doorstep, where I spent the best thirteen years of my professional career.

Following a weekend retreat in 1975, Doug Baker and I formed a True North Group. We didn't call it that in those days; instead, it was our "renewal group" that enabled us to renew ourselves each week. In 1983, we also formed a couples group of eight that includes our spouses and two other couples who are close friends.

In addition to my wife, Penny's, love and counsel, the people in these two groups have done more to help me develop as a whole human being and an authentic leader than anything else in my life. They have helped increase my self-awareness, sensitivity to others, and self-acceptance.

In the early years, they helped me recognize I was trying so hard to get ahead that I was behaving very differently in my work and community than at home and in my personal life. That led me to "decompartmentalize" my life by attempting to be the same person at home, at work, and in the community—with less facade and more authenticity.

When I hit the wall in my Honeywell career—something most of us have to confront at some point—our men's group helped me acknowledge that I was striving too hard to become CEO and was in danger of losing sight of my True North. Back in 1988, I was on the fast track to the top of Honeywell. Elected executive vice president in 1983, I took over a large organization where I discovered lots of problems as I dug deeply into each of the businesses.

Just as we were getting these businesses in shape, I was asked to take over a new set of businesses and get them turned around. In late 1987, I was given responsibility for the third major turnaround, where we uncovered nearly $500 million in cost overruns on fixed-price government contracts that had to be written off.

One day in 1988, I was driving home on a beautiful fall day when I looked at myself in the mirror and realized I was deeply unhappy. In that instant flash in the mirror, I recognized that I was losing sight of my True North. I was striving so hard to get to the top that I was moving away from being an inspirational, growth-oriented leader. When I told Penny what I was feeling, she said, "Bill, I have been trying to tell you that for the past year, but you didn't want to listen." Often it is the people closest to us who see us as we are and can recognize our blind spots.

The next morning I shared my feelings with our group. They were helpful in confirming the changes they had seen in me and sharing their perceptions about my growing unhappiness. They suggested I rethink the opportunity to join Medtronic that I had turned down the previous summer. Later that week, I called Medtronic back, which opened up the best move of my career—one that I couldn't see without the help of my wife and my men's group.

In 1996, Penny was diagnosed with breast cancer. I'll never forget our couples group sitting together beneath the surgical room at Abbott Northwestern Hospital while she was having her mastectomy. Even with that support, I struggled to face the risks Penny faced and to share her fears. My men's group pointed out that I seemed to be in denial about the uncertainty of her health, probably due to losing both my mother and my first fiancée to cancer early in life. That allowed me to stop trying to "fix it" and to just be a support person for Penny, an entirely new role for me.

Ten years ago, I concluded my business career and went on a wilderness journey to contemplate what lay ahead. Whatever I explored—from health care to international relations, corporate governance, government service, and education—my thoughts always came back to leadership.

Thanks to the trauma associated with the fall of Enron and dozens of companies whose executives got them into trouble, I found a new calling in helping others become more authentic leaders—from my MBA students to CEOs. Through this experience, I learned I could have greater impact in helping others lead effectively than I could in leading myself. As I wrote *Authentic Leadership, True North,* and two other books on leadership, I realized that my thesis is always the same: we need a new generation of authentic leaders to become values-centered leaders guiding great organizations.

After retiring from Medtronic and spending two years teaching in Switzerland and at Yale School of Management, I joined the faculty of Harvard Business School in 2004 to teach a new course called Leadership and Corporate Accountability. I soon realized there was an absence of leadership development courses for MBA students.

In interviewing leaders in 2005–06 for *True North* and reviewing transcripts from 125 leaders, our research team concluded that one of the keys to sustaining your leadership is having a support team around you. In addition to your spouse, partner, or mentor, we recognized that a support group was the most important thing people could do to stay grounded and increase their self-awareness.

In 2005, I introduced a new elective course at Harvard Business School called Authentic Leadership Development. To encourage greater intimacy and more opportunities for personal sharing, we created six-person groups, modeled after our men's group. These groups are identical to the True North Groups described in these pages. The group meetings are official classes, accounting for 50 percent of the course. Unique in the Harvard Business School curriculum, these small groups are consistently rated by MBAs as the course's highlight and one of the most important experiences in their MBA programs.

In the past seven years, more than 1,100 Harvard MBAs have participated in these groups. Due to the course's popularity, the school is considering broadening its availability to all students. Most recently, we introduced a five-day version of the course for senior executives. In their evaluations, the participants were uniformly enthusiastic about their small, six-person groups. They scored the small groups higher than any other aspect of the course, saying they were the most valuable part of their experience. It was remarkable that this could happen in just five days, especially since they had never met the people in their group before the program.

True North Groups have also been used successfully by the Young Global Leaders of the World Economic Forum, global corporations, and other educational institutions, such as New York University and Georgia Tech. Similar groups, like the Forum of the Young Presidents' Organization, have operated successfully for decades.

Personally, I am very excited about the possibility of many more people creating True North Groups and having similar opportunities for intimacy, sharing, personal growth, and leadership development.

DOUG'S STORY

My introduction to groups was with athletic teams that lacked cohesiveness. As a college player and assistant coach, I saw our head coach bring a bunch of wildly independent athletes into a semblance of teamwork. Yet, with few exceptions, we were never close friends.

Then, as a young Army company commander, I watched my experienced first sergeant recruit a strong team of noncommissioned officers that helped build our unit into an award-winning unit. Away from the job, few were close pals.

At the Pillsbury Company, I was introduced to early organizational and leadership development practices that stimulated me to pursue this line of work in my career. As a teacher, consultant, and corporate executive, I have worked to bring increased effectiveness to multiple organizations and people. Even so, few of these groups and teams had the intimacy and bonding to move beyond work relationships. I believed that a different and deeper relationship among team members would produce better results.

During these early years, Bill and I—along with two friends, Tom Schaefer and Gordy Lund—formed the men's group that continues to this day. As some of the original members moved away, we carefully introduced new members into the group. Today there are eight of us, all of whom have been part of the group for the past fifteen years.

As we matured and began to delve into more personal issues, the bonds deepened and grew richer. We experienced the joys and heartbreaks of life: loss of a child; death of a member; divorce; birth of children and grandchildren and their graduations and marriages; career successes and some failures; and health issues, both our own and in our families. We came to rely on the support of our members to help carry us through these challenges. Our bonding and intimacy, coupled with our joint search for answers to life's mysteries, proved the value of a closer, more entwined group.

For me personally, these men helped further shape my ethical boundaries. After leaving Pillsbury, I became a partner of a consulting group. After two years, we discovered one of the partners was having an extramarital affair with one of our contract trainers and was covering up some of her unprofessional training methods, one of which caused harm to my wife, Carole. My initial attempts to have this trainer removed were unsuccessful. I went to our group to ask if I was on a valid course and they recommended that I should bring the matter to a head. Unable to force the resignation of the part-ner who was involved with the trainer, I left the firm.

Another time, the group pushed me to tackle a signifi-cant problem with my back rather than continuing alterna-tive approaches. They also suggested the surgeon who helped me greatly.

Still later, the group helped me wrestle with an offer to take a senior position in New York City with American Express. After listening to my summary of the opportunity and the strong objections of my wife, the group unanimously advised me to turn the opportunity down. They felt I did not respond well to the stresses of big corporations and that my marriage was too important to ignore Carole's wishes. I fol-lowed their advice, took early retirement from corporate life at age 55, and have enjoyed coaching, writing, teaching, and traveling ever since.

The counsel and support I received are not unusual for friends to provide, but the variety of perspectives that improves the judgment of our group and its collective wis-dom lends the power of numbers to the advice. Most help-ful of all has been their feedback about my tendencies and style that often hindered my effectiveness as a leader. When I heard these things from these people who had my best inter-ests at heart, it was impossible to ignore their suggestions.

About ten years ago, I decided I wanted to share the value of our group with others. Starting with the base of some cli-ents of my coaching practice, I began to form groups using our True North Group model and the techniques we recom-mend in this book. My colleagues and I have started eight groups, with others currently in the formative stage. Some of their stories appear later in the book.

What impresses me about the True North Group process is the enormous benefit of examining our lives in great detail and receiving encouragement to continue to grow and evolve. Our group provides solid, supportive feedback about how we come across to others. We have a chance to test our assumptions and beliefs and to make necessary changes as we learn more about ourselves, others, and the world. Over time, we expand our self-awareness into self-acceptance. In all of this, I have become a more effective leader in my groups, on the boards I serve, in my community, and in my family.

WHAT CAN A TRUE NORTH GROUP MEAN FOR YOU?

Having worked together in groups for thirty-six years, we have often talked about writing a book on small groups that could help others find the same joy, intimacy, and support we have in our groups. Those talks became the genesis of this book. We have written *True North Groups* to help you form such a group or revitalize your existing group.

Our research on groups and our personal interviews with fifty-two group members, described in Resource 12, gave us useful insights that we share in these pages. The quotes in the book come directly from those interviews. Building on this research and our personal experiences with groups, *True North Groups* describes how to build a successful group and what it can mean to you.

Ask yourself: Where do you go for advice and perspective when facing difficult decisions? Who can you count on to help you through the most challenging times? Who will be honest enough to point out your blind spots? Who would you talk to if you lost your job, your marriage were falling apart, or you faced a life-threatening illness?

Your True North Group can do all of these things—and more. It can help you sort out your values, your priorities, and your beliefs. It can give you insights about yourself that will enhance your self-awareness and enable you to live authentically. And it can enable you to build deep, lasting friendships.

Your group can help you fill the void you may feel in your life by having people to talk to whom you can trust. In spite of being members of families, organizations where we work, communities where we live, and faith-based bodies where we worship, often there is no one we feel comfortable with in sharing the most important details of our lives. Unless we have people around us with whom we can be completely honest and open, it is surprising just how alone we can feel in our work, and even at home.

As a leader, being part of a True North Group provides you with constructive feedback on a regular basis from people who know you well. It offers a place to refine your authentic approach to leading and to sharpen your skills as a facilitator. As one interviewee observed, these groups are a place to get frequent, 360-degree feedback from people whose motives you trust completely.

THE BROADER NEED FOR PERSONAL GROUPS

In his 2000 book *Bowling Alone,* author Robert Putnam describes the demise of groups in contemporary society. He presents convincing evidence that the organizations our parents joined for camaraderie are in a stage of decline. Nor have they been replaced by newer organizations that fill our need for deeper relationships. Putnam writes, "Most Americans today feel vaguely and uncomfortably disconnected."[2]

The irony is that we are surrounded by people—lots of them—all the time. These days it is actually hard to be by yourself. But we often feel alone in the midst of the turmoil, difficulties, and challenges of our everyday lives. The demise of group affiliations has left many of us feeling trapped in trying to navigate life's challenges on our own. Yet we long for opportunities to share who we are, our life stories, and the great questions we have about life.

Sociologists report that most of us have about 150 friends, people we see from time to time. Many of them are acquaintances, not close friends. Similarly, neighbors or people we work with on PTA committees probably aren't those with whom we would share an important decision in our lives. If we're honest with ourselves about how many intimate friends we have—those people with whom we would share our most personal dilemmas—we can count them on the fingers of one hand. When asked in 2004 by social researchers how many confidantes they had, 25 percent of Americans said they had none.

Our desire to be fiercely independent often keeps us from developing the close relationships we need to journey joyfully through life. In their 2008 book *Loneliness*, social neuroscientist John Cacioppo and co-author William Patrick suggest that "our society may have gone overboard in its emphasis on standing alone." They assert,

> We pay the price, not just in terms of our mental and physical health, but in terms of the strain on social cohesion . . . Independence is the rallying point for our culture . . . However, that swashbuckling independence could be better described as rootlessness . . . Feelings of social isolation deprive us of vast reservoirs of creativity and energy. Connection adds more water to the well that nourishes our human potential.[3]

There is a paradox in our individualism. We are spending more time than ever before in organizations where we work, yet the organizations in which we participate are ever larger and more impersonal. Few of the relationships formed in these organizations provide opportunities for depth, openness, authenticity, or personal development.

In response to these trends, many people have searched for ways to develop themselves individually. In recent decades, opportunities for personal development have proliferated, from the flourishing of yoga and Pilates courses, fitness centers, and adult education classes to individual therapy sessions. While these vehicles provide opportunities for personal development, they do not address the gnawing need we have for depth and intimacy in our interactions with others.

In working on our personal development, we often discover deep conflicts between our personal desires and the expectations of our organizations. Yet we don't know how to resolve these conflicts, nor do we have a safe place to discuss them. As a result, we feel a growing isolation within our organizations.

Navigating life's challenges on our own is risky. All of us have blind spots that prevent us from seeing ourselves as we are. Often we lack perspective on the questions we are facing. Left to ourselves, with no counsel or advice, we are prone to making bad decisions. Sometimes we cannot face our own reality. Instead of looking at ourselves in the mirror, we blame others for our difficulties. Without people we trust to point out our blind spots, we may be attempting to journey through life without recognizing our shortcomings or seeing ourselves as others see us.

Commenting on the importance of small groups, organization consultant Maureen Swan says, "The notion that you can develop yourself alone is false." She explains,

> We need the intimacy of a small group and the feedback to create a mirror to reflect where we're at. When you try to do it alone, you don't have the opportunity for reflection that happens in a small group. You can look inside yourself in a different way because you have individuals around that you can learn from. It's so much different than a book club.

THE FACEBOOK PHENOMENON

To fill these gaps, Web-based social media sites like Facebook, Twitter, and LinkedIn have exploded in membership in the past five years. Today, Facebook has over six hundred million registered users and was recently valued at $50 billion, making it one of the most valuable companies in the world. Twitter has grown to more than two hundred fifty million users and is adding fifteen million new users every month. Many people assume this explosive growth is being driven by the millennial generation, yet the most rapidly growing demographic on Facebook today is people over forty.

Social media sites are an excellent way for us to reconnect with our old acquaintances and to meet new ones. They offer opportunities to link to lots of people, many of whom we have never met in person. Simply by pushing Enter on our computer keyboard, we can communicate with hundreds, even thousands of people in our extended network.

Bill is an active user of social media. He sends daily messages about contemporary leadership issues to a network of 10,000 people, which generates some interesting dialogues about these issues. But, for him, social media are certainly not a substitute for trusting relationships where he can discuss his most difficult challenges. Social media outlets cannot provide this level of intimacy, confidentiality, or opportunities for in-depth discussion, any more than the Lion's Club or a social group can.

TRUE NORTH GROUPS

This book is written with a dual purpose. The first is to demonstrate how rewarding it is to have a True North Group. You will learn about the inspiring stories of people who have participated in groups and what they got out of them. From our interviews with group members, we learned that most people yearn for friendships and relationships with people they can trust and admire. They are eager to have a place where they can discuss their issues, their hopes, and their dreams. They hunger for that kind of intimacy but don't know where to find it.

The second purpose is to provide you with a manual that guides the formation of your True North Group. The book will help you organize your group to ensure its success, and includes a complete set of programs for the first year and many program ideas beyond the start-up phase.

In these pages we will attempt to answer questions like these:

- How can a True North Group help you steer between your personal life and the larger world you confront every day?
- How can your group help you develop as a person and become a more effective leader?
- What is required for your group to be fulfilling and rewarding for everyone in it?
- What processes are needed to keep your group alive and vital?
- Why are some groups successful, while others fall apart?
- How can you deal with the inevitable interpersonal difficulties that will confront your group?

THE STAGES OF A GROUP'S LIFE

True North Groups is organized around a familiar sequence that is common to groups: *forming, norming, storming, performing,* and *reforming.* This progression for group development was originally developed by Bruce Tuckman in 1965.[4] For our purposes, we change Tuckman's sequence because we prefer to address norming before storming, as the former is a way to prevent the latter. We have added the fifth stage, reforming.

Chapter 1 offers a complete introduction to True North Groups and how they can work for you. In Chapter 2, we examine the vital role True North Groups can play in your personal and leadership development. Then we move to the first stage, *forming*, which encompasses all the elements you need to create a True North Group, along with suggestions to ensure the building of a sound foundation for your group.

Perhaps the least obvious of the stages, *norming* is the creation of habits, practices, and rules characterizing your group's behavior and the ways in which your group members interact. Although people can describe the group's tangible norms, the more subtle — and often more important — norms may be less apparent and can escape observation except by a trained observer.

The *storming* phase describes the disagreements that your members may have with each other individually and often with the group as a whole. Storms can be well concealed for some time and then break out as highly visible and verbal disputes. In many ways, storms within your group may be inevitable if you have people who are passionate about life and the topics being discussed. It is the effective handling of these episodes that will determine your group's longevity and the long-term satisfaction of your members.

Performing covers the period when your group is operating productively. This is the groove that every group seeks to achieve. In discussing this phase, we suggest programs for the first year of a group's existence that will give the group both depth and substance and provide the basis for intimate discussions.

The final stage, *reforming*, usually comes later in a group's life, when the group needs to reshape itself in order to provide ongoing satisfaction for its members, and sustainability.

In the event the members decide that reforming is not possible, we provide suggestions for disbanding the group gracefully.

We describe these stages as if each is a separate and distinct set of activities. Although this linear approach helps clarify them, the stages do not always fit neatly in this order. It is not unusual, for example, to have some early storming while membership issues are being hashed out. The same can occur while trying to set norms for the new group, especially if attendance standards are used. Norming starts early in formation, with consideration of the group's purpose and decisions about the members to include. Reforming occurs whenever new members are invited to join the group or existing members leave.

The Resources section offers a manual of the tools needed to develop the group, including a curriculum with the first twelve recommended topics and an additional thirty-five ideas for dynamic programs.

We hope you will form or create a True North Group and learn how it can transform your life and enable you to be more fulfilled.

CHAPTER 1

True North Groups

IN THE INTRODUCTION, WE EXAMINED THE BENEFITS of having a small, intimate group in our lives to support us during challenging times and enable us to live lives of joy and fulfillment. Let's begin by focusing on what True North Groups are and how they work.

TRUE NORTH GROUPS

What is a True North Group? It consists of six to eight people who meet on a regular basis to share their personal challenges and discuss important questions in their lives. At various times your True North Group will function as a nurturer, a grounding rod, a truth teller, and a mirror. At other times the group functions as a challenger or an inspirer. At their best, the members of your group serve each other as caring coaches and thoughtful mentors.

Your True North Group is characterized by high levels of trust between your members, something that may be hard to find at work or even in your community. When you feel self-doubts, your group helps build the courage and ability to cope. The trust of your group enables all members to be open and intimate, building on your shared commitment to maintain strict confidentiality.

Your group will stimulate your beliefs about the important issues of life and help you think through the challenges you face. Group members will give you constructive feedback when you need it most. Most importantly, your group is a safe haven when you are facing difficult times and experiencing stress and distress—something all of us encounter from time to time.

OUR TRUE NORTH GROUP

To get a better understanding of what a True North Group is and how it operates, let's take an in-depth look at the group we formed in the spring of 1975. The eight of us had participated in a retreat weekend and were searching for ways to continue the openness, sharing, and intimacy we had experienced.

We decided to meet weekly in the living room of a neighborhood church on Wednesday mornings from 7:15 to 8:30 a.m. Thirty-six years later, the group meets every Wednesday in that same place. Three members of our original group are still active and the others have joined us over the years. One of our members died, another got divorced and moved away, and the others were transferred out of town.

Our current group includes two lawyers, five businessmen, and an architect. Each person brings to the group a unique perspective on life, on beliefs, and on human nature. In spite of significant differences in our faiths and beliefs, we have a common commitment to sharing our lives openly, respecting our differences, and discussing the challenges and difficulties we face.

The Group's Importance to Our Members

What's the glue that has kept the group together all these years? Group member Peter Gillette, former president of a large bank, says, "It's one of those mysterious combinations of the people, setting, experiences, mutual respect, and humor."

> The flexibility of our topics makes it conducive for all elements of personality and articulation to thrive. There is a bonding, camaraderie, and trust. It's the differences between us that provide the spark that makes the conversation so stimulating.

Business executive Tom Schaefer explains, "Our group has become the most important community in my life, other than my immediate family." He adds,

> It's a community of seven brothers that has helped guide my life in terms of spiritual formation, work, and personal growth. It continually challenges my beliefs about life, values, and spirit. It provides a safe place where I can examine these issues, reflect on them, and understand what others feel about such important matters. These guys operate as my special board of advisors, as they provide a lot of life coaching.
>
> Our group was so important that there were times I left my job in part to stay with the group rather than move out of town. I knew I couldn't duplicate it somewhere else and didn't want to give it up. I've always wanted to feel proud of my work and my actions in front of my pals, so I ask myself how the group would react about something I'm considering. It provides a moral compass, a way of checking on my sense of what's right and wrong.

The Group's Process

As we gather each week, we have a brief check-in to enable people to bring up anything significant in their lives. Then one of us initiates discussion of the program. Responsibility for leading the program is rotated every two weeks, so each of us takes the lead about six times a year.

Although many groups may choose to hire their own professional facilitator to prepare programs and lead discussions, our group prefers having our members take responsibility for facilitating, to ensure everyone feels equal responsibility for the group. (See Resource 7 for a complete discussion of facilitator options.) Attorney Ron Vantine explains, "We decided not to have an expert or a full-time facilitator because we didn't want to look to an expert for the answers. Instead, we wanted to come up with questions that were crucial to us."

On a regular basis, we take a check to be sure that everyone in the group is feeling satisfied and fulfilled. Periodically, we ask ourselves, How are we doing? Are we getting out of our heads and into our hearts and souls? Each of us does that to varying degrees. Some of us are better at asking questions and guiding the conversation; others excel at giving small seminars.

Addressing Life's Most Important Questions

Our group provides opportunities to challenge our views and grow from the questions. Chuck Denny, former CEO of a large telecommunications company, highlights the importance of deep discussions: "We talk about our values and where they come from." He asks,

> What has been their importance in our lives? Have they been tested? Do we stay true to them under stress? It's introspective, not just intellectual. What are we doing to make society better? How do we allocate time between ourselves, our family, and society? These discussions have helped me create the road map for each phase of my life.

Architect John Cuningham says, "At some point in their lives everybody asks the big questions like Why am I here? What is life all about? What is my purpose?" He says,

> Our group has grappled with these questions through happy and sad experiences. There is no judgment and no critical analysis of our beliefs. We have struggled with them in our personal spiritual journeys, as we move in and out of doubt about what we believe. The questions never seem to change, but the answers are different when you're 69 than when you're 39.

Opening Up and Sharing Intimately

Over the years, we have built relationships of trust and intimacy. Vantine notes, "The group enriches my life and my understanding of what I want out of life and what I can contribute. The discussions make me feel my values are worthy because they are shared by other men I admire and respect." He explains,

> These conversations are much different than ones with social friends, colleagues at work, or even family members. I know only a couple of men where I can get to such a level of depth. With us, it happens every week. That's because we have the trust, environment, and relationships that have built up over all these years. The group has a unique place in my life.
>
> There is never a clash of egos in our group. None of us feel we have to prove anything to the rest of the group. If that happened, the person would be called on it. None of us is trying to impress the others with our titles, power, and influence, or suggest that we have all the answers. We all have more questions than answers.

It wasn't always this way. It took a number of years to let go of our egos and to be willing to share our weaknesses and vulnerabilities. Typically, we find that it takes men longer than women to break through their defenses to become more reflective and less defensive.

Vantine adds, "There are few places in life where I have a chance to talk about significant issues, particularly things that are personal. It's unusual to get into those topics in an environment where everyone feels secure, has a high level of trust, and wants to learn from each other."

What are the benefits of this level of intimacy and openness? St. Paul attorney Jonathan Morgan says, "The group provides a venue for discussing existential questions and life's mysteries that stretches the mind almost to the breaking point."

> We share our challenges, obstacles, joys, and times of sadness. We're there to help and support each other and offer prayers and benedictions for each other. The collegiality and trust that have developed give the group sustaining power.

Tom Schaefer observes, "Learning I could ask for help was a huge leap for me."

> A big part of my growth has been learning I don't have to have all the answers and can't figure it all out by myself. I found out everybody needs help at various times. Learning to be vulnerable in this group has enabled me to be vulnerable elsewhere.

Experiencing Life's Challenges

Longevity also has its rewards. Together we have shared our life stories, both when we met and as we experience life's challenges. Collectively, our lives are enriched by sharing the full range of life's joys and sorrows. From the combined experiences of people who have been through all these things has developed a collective wisdom in our group. This results from trusting relationships and the acceptance of each person for who he is.

Chuck Denny described the group's importance to his coping with his wife, Carol's, descent into the darkness of Alzheimer's disease. "The group gave me incredible support in those years when I was caring for Carol at home."

> I could acknowledge to the group just how difficult and tiring this was and what it was like to feel socially isolated. Being together each week enabled me to banter with humor with a group of trusted friends. It provided a social contribution that filled a void in my life because I couldn't go out. Wednesday mornings are a sacred time, not in a spiritual sense but in finding nourishment, support, acceptance, and an hour of fun.

Tom Schaefer described how the group helped him face a difficult ethical challenge. "As chief financial officer for a manufacturing business, I discovered we were repackaging returned goods and selling them as new."

> I told the group I felt this was an ethical crossroads for me, and they affirmed my concerns. As a result, I told the owner I couldn't live with this practice. He agreed, and we ended up stopping the repackaging.

Reflections on the Group

We frequently ask ourselves, Is there something unique about the eight of us that makes this group work so well and stay together for so many years? We don't think we are different than any eight people who genuinely want to explore together the important questions of their lives. What is crucial is the willingness of each of us to share openly, join in the give-and-take of a peer group, and listen in a nonjudgmental way to the challenges others face.

THE EMERGENCE OF SMALL GROUPS

Small groups are certainly not a new phenomenon. We learned through our field research that participation in small groups is gaining strength. These groups arise both formally and informally and have many different purposes. Most people have participated in one kind of group or another.

In doing the research for this book (see Resource 12), we examined many of these groups to understand how they operate and what makes them successful. Examples of the types of groups we explored include:

- Book and study groups
- Prayer groups, Bible study, and other religious groups
- Alcoholics Anonymous groups
- Twelve-step groups that focus on other addictions
- Cooking groups, bridge groups, and wine tasting groups
- Therapy groups, grief groups, and other support groups
- The Forum of the Young Presidents' Organization
- Small groups within companies
- Travel groups
- Biking, walking, running, and golf groups

These groups are affinity groups whose members come together around a common set of interests or a common concern such as chemical dependency, life-threatening illness, or loss of loved ones. Those interests and concerns provide the focal point for the group's programs or meetings. Typically,

EXHIBIT I

Openness and Intimacy of Groups

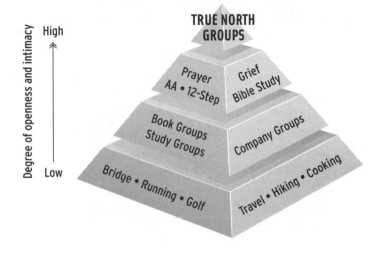

Degree of openness and intimacy

High

Low

TRUE NORTH GROUPS

Prayer
AA • 12-Step

Grief
Bible Study

Book Groups
Study Groups

Company Groups

Bridge • Running • Golf

Travel • Hiking • Cooking

the members take turns leading their groups, whether by proposing menus for a cooking group, studying biblical passages for a Bible study group, or planning routes for a biking trip.

One way of categorizing small groups is by their degree of openness and intimacy. At the base of the pyramid are travel, running, cooking, or bridge groups, and so forth (see Exhibit 1). People in these groups come together for an activity rather than for personal sharing. To the extent that there are personal discussions, it is independent of or incidental to the group's activities. At the next level are book groups, study groups, and company groups that have intellectual discussions that occasionally delve into personal matters, depending on the topic of the group.

On the third level are Bible study groups, prayer groups,

grief groups, therapy groups, Alcoholics Anonymous, and twelve-step groups that are affiliated around a particular purpose and share deeply about that area, including discussions of personal feelings, convictions, and beliefs. Many prayer groups and Bible study groups offer their members opportunities for examination of their religious beliefs and provide strong bonding around shared values.

True North Groups, as described in this book, provide a forum for deep, intimate discussions of all aspects of one's life, not only matters of belief and faith. These may include personal issues, such as family problems, leadership and career concerns, or healthy living, as well as convictions about a wide spectrum of subjects. They are fairly unique in providing a safe place for confidential discussions of highly personal subjects across the full range of life's issues, but without any particular affinity.

THE CELLULAR CHURCH

Before exploring True North Groups, it may be useful to look more closely at one kind of upper-tier organization that is growing rapidly—megachurches like Rick Warren's Saddleback Church, the largest in the United States. In 2005 Malcolm Gladwell, author of *The Tipping Point*, wrote a widely read article for *The New Yorker* called "The Cellular Church." In the article, he compared small groups in megachurches like Saddleback to cells in a larger organism. Gladwell describes how Warren created "a church out of a network of lots of little church cells—exclusive, tightly knit groups of six or seven who meet in one another's homes during the week to worship and pray." He writes,

> The small group as an instrument of community is
> initially how Communism spread, and in the postwar

years Alcoholics Anonymous and its twelve-step progeny perfected the small-group technique. The small group did not have a designated leader who stood at the front of the room. Members sat in a circle. The focus was on discussion and interaction—not one person teaching and the others listening—and the remarkable thing about these groups was their power. An alcoholic could lose his job and his family, he could be hospitalized, he could be warned by half a dozen doctors—and go on drinking. But put him in a room of his peers once a week—make him share the burdens of others and have his burdens shared by others—and he could do something that once seemed impossible.[5]

Gladwell explains that megachurches adopted the cellular model because they found that "the small group was an extraordinary vehicle of commitment." He writes,

It was personal and flexible. It cost nothing. It was convenient, and every worshipper was able to find a small group that precisely matched his or her interests. Today, at least forty million Americans are in a religiously based small group, and the growing ranks of small-group membership have caused a profound shift in the nature of the American religious experience.

Intrigued by the rapid expansion of the membership of these churches, Bill visited Willow Creek in a Chicago suburb in 2008 to meet with Pastor Bill Hybels. Mystified about how people could feel at home with 22,000 people attending weekly worship services, Bill was told, "We are a community of small groups who meet weekly to discuss the Bible and its impact on our lives, and then we all worship together on weekends."[6]

WHY TRUE NORTH GROUPS ARE DIFFERENT

True North Groups are not built around affinity models that provide the glue that brings them together and gives their members opportunities for sharing common interests. Our research confirmed that no prior bond is required for a True North Group; in fact, a diverse set of strangers is just as effective as preexisting affinity among members. They often have no particular connection except the longing for affiliation, openness, and commitment to personal growth and leadership development.

In offering opportunities for deep discussions about challenges people face, True North Groups provide a safe place where members can discuss personal issues they do not feel they can raise elsewhere—often not even with their closest family members—and can explore questions about the meaning and purpose of life.

For example, one group member told us he had shared with his colleagues his agony about whether to separate from his wife. He said the group helped him recognize his dissatisfaction resulted more from his issues than his wife's. After months of discussions with his group and assistance from a professional counselor, he and his wife are back together and seem satisfied with their relationship.

After working closely with dozens of groups, participating in several groups ourselves, and researching the small group phenomenon, we conclude that True North Groups are one of the best opportunities individuals have to grow as human beings and leaders and to develop their full potential.

CHAPTER 2

Your Personal and Leadership Development

NOW WE TURN OUR ATTENTION TO THE QUESTION OF *how* True North Groups can help you grow as a human being and develop as a leader. By offering a simple structure accessible to a wide range of individuals, your group provides the opportunity to explore your life, your beliefs, and your values more deeply. In doing so, it offers a powerful path between your personal life and the larger organizations you are part of, and supports your leadership roles.

First, some context. As a result of myriad leadership and economic failures in the past, both personal growth and leadership development are undergoing a significant rethinking. Macroeconomic theories prevalent for the past thirty years convinced many opinion leaders that people are motivated by monetary gains alone and act only in their economic self-interest.

As a result of economic difficulties in the first ten years of the twenty-first century, these theories are being widely challenged. This is triggering a reassessment of the limits and importance of monetary gains. More importantly, it is rekindling desires to find a deeper sense of purpose and meaning in life.

REVISITING OUR HUMAN NEEDS AND DRIVES

Psychologists have known for decades that monetary accumulation and material possessions are only one of our drives. In 1943, Brandeis University Professor Abraham Maslow, founder of humanistic psychology, published his paper on the hierarchy of needs.[7] He identified five levels of human needs (Exhibit 2).

Maslow postulated that human beings need to satisfy their more basic needs, such as physiological and safety needs, before they can focus on higher-order needs like love/belonging, esteem, and self-actualization. We have learned in the past that society's overemphasis on one aspect of needs—resources and money—has created a void in our society because higher-order needs are not being addressed.

A close friend of Bill's who works with wealthy young people reports that many of them feel a deep hollowness inside. Having acquired all the material possessions they could ever use—and more—they ask, Is this all there is? His honest answer is, If all you're chasing is money and what it will buy you, then yes, that's all there is.

Of course, there is so much more to life than money and its rewards. As human beings, we have a deep need to be loved by our family and friends and to experience intimacy in those relationships. We also crave self-esteem, self-confidence, the respect of others, and the ability to achieve things we deem worthwhile. At our highest level of need, we desire to think of ourselves as moral individuals who respect all human beings and can use our leadership to help others and better humanity.

True North Groups provide a safe place where we can explore the higher levels of Maslow's hierarchy—love/belonging, esteem, and self-actualization. As people learn that material acquisitions alone cannot satisfy them, they are

EXHIBIT 2

Maslow's Hierarchy of Needs

LEVEL	CATEGORY
1	**Physiological**
	air · water · food · sleep · sex
2	**Safety**
	security · employment · resources · health
3	**Love/belonging**
	friendship · family · intimacy
4	**Esteem**
	confidence · respect · achievement
5	**Self-actualization**
	morality · creativity · accepting reality

turning to small groups to address these needs and to understand the meaning of their lives.

True North Groups enable us to integrate these drives for bonding and comprehension into our development as human beings and leaders. In these groups there is no threat of being judged by peers, superiors, or society in general. Consulting executive Maureen Swan believes a True North Group is "a place where life gets real. It causes me to ask questions about how we can live our lives safely and helpfully, and how we can help others to grow."

Ron Vantine talked about the role of group discussions in broadening his thinking about these essential issues. "We frequently talk about our values, habits, and beliefs," he said.

As I learn more about these factors in other people's lives, I learn different perspectives on a wide range of topics. In that process, my worldview expands beyond what I previously perceived or believed.

EMOTIONAL INTELLIGENCE

An important aspect of the growth experience in True North Groups is the development of emotional intelligence (EQ) — the ability to identify, assess, and control one's emotions. The roots of EQ can be traced to Charles Darwin's work on the importance of emotional expression for survival and adaptation to one's environment.

In his 1998 book *Working with Emotional Intelligence,* psychologist Daniel Goleman defined EQ as a set of competencies that drives leadership performance.[8] His model includes:

- *Self-awareness:* the ability to read one's emotions and recognize their impact
- *Self-management:* controlling one's emotions and impulses and adapting to changing circumstances
- *Social awareness:* the ability to sense, understand, and react to others' emotions while comprehending social networks
- *Relationship management:* the ability to inspire, influence, and develop others while managing conflict

Goleman believes individuals are born with a general emotional intelligence that determines their potential for learning emotional competencies. However, he says EQ competencies are *not* innate talents but rather are learned capabilities that can be developed to achieve outstanding performance.

EXHIBIT 3

The Path to Self-actualization

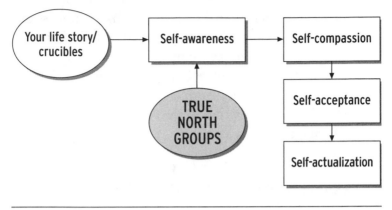

TRUE NORTH GROUPS AND THE DEVELOPMENT OF EMOTIONAL INTELLIGENCE

Self-awareness may be the key to EQ, but gaining it is more difficult than it seems. In our experience, becoming self-aware requires three things:

- *Experience* in real-world situations, including opportunities for leadership
- *Reflection* about your experiences and the ability to process objectively what you did well and what you need to improve
- *Group interactions* that can provide a place to share your experiences and get honest feedback about yourself

True North Groups are most effective in the third category. They provide the feedback that enables people to understand their blind spots, open up hidden areas, and gain a deeper understanding of who they are at their core. In so doing, they offer a unique environment for people to develop their self-awareness, self-compassion, and authenticity.

Having self-awareness enables people to have compassion for themselves. Without self-compassion, it is difficult, if not impossible, to have genuine compassion for other people and the difficulties they may be facing. Self-compassion also leads to self-acceptance and, ultimately, to self-actualization (see Exhibit 3). These qualities are essential to sustaining your authenticity as a leader.

RETHINKING LEADERSHIP AND THE DEVELOPMENT OF LEADERS

Just as human motivation is being reinterpreted, leadership development is also being rethought. With multiple failures of command-and-control structures and top-down leadership styles, organizations are recognizing the need to develop a new generation of leaders who can lead effectively in the twenty-first century.

Progressive organizations need inner-directed leaders who have the necessary capabilities to empower their people at all levels to step up and lead. They need leaders who can align people around the organization's mission and values, empower other people instead of exerting power over them, act as servant leaders, and collaborate throughout the organization.

This is a much different profile than the authoritarian style so prevalent among twentieth-century leaders. It raises two vital questions about leadership development:

- How can organizations develop inner-directed leaders?
- How can they create development programs for large

numbers of people instead of intensive programs for a few select leaders?

Before those questions can be answered, it is essential to get to the root cause of myriad leadership failures in the past decade. In our experience, we have never seen leaders fail for lack of raw intelligence. However, we have observed and worked with many leaders who have failed for lack of emotional intelligence.

Goleman explains, "High levels of cognitive ability (i.e., measured IQ of 120 or greater) are a threshold qualification for leadership roles. Once you are at or above that level, IQ loses power as a predictor of success. EQ then plays a larger role."[9] His conclusion was confirmed by a recent Egon Zehnder International study of executives who failed.

As David Gergen, director of the Center for Public Leadership at Harvard Kennedy School, writes in the Foreword to *True North*, "Growing up in the shadow of a great university, I always believed the smartest person made the best leader."

> I just assumed that smart people were the best at most things, including leadership. Boy, did I have some things to learn. . . . What ultimately distinguishes the great leaders from the mediocre are the personal, inner qualities—qualities that are hard to define but are essential for success.[10]

If emotional intelligence is the single most important determinant of leadership effectiveness, then how can we develop our EQ? This is where True North Groups become so valuable in leadership development. Our research and personal experiences indicate that being part of an ongoing group of six people who know you intimately is the best way to develop your EQ.

Leadership development consultant Dr. Kathryn Williams describes the role of small groups in her work in leadership development. She says, "For development of leaders or people, group work is the best technique. Groups accelerate people's ability to better understand themselves and identify with others. Through the group experience people can be given honest feedback in a way that is not destructive."

In working with True North Groups, we have learned the added benefits of having feedback from the multiple perspectives of peers within the group. This approach is more likely to enable individuals to absorb the feedback and use it to develop themselves than is feedback from a boss or someone who individuals may not be convinced has their best interests at heart.

Digging into why a True North Group has been so important to her leadership development, Maureen Swan concludes, "The small group is a place where you get to know who you are."

> My group causes me to reflect on where I am in my development. It enables me to be a better leader and understand what gets in my way of being effective. It's much easier to do this in a small group than it is in the work world. I need to share with the group what I don't know, which is difficult for leaders to acknowledge in themselves.

As the limitations of leaders at the top have become apparent, there is growing recognition of the importance of developing leaders at all levels, even those with no direct reports. Consequently, organizations need to develop a much broader array of leaders than in the past, when they focused on a few select leaders. True North Groups can help to fill this gap in leadership development. There is essentially no cost to these groups, no professional leaders are required, and limited staff is needed to support them. In this sense, they are scalable for organizations that want to use True North Groups to develop large numbers of leaders.

In interviewing 125 authentic leaders for *True North,* our research team learned that the most important characteristic of sustained, effective leadership is the ability to stay grounded. By that, we mean the capacity to absorb pressure, make clear, logical decisions, and not let your success, power, or prestige go to your head.

In a small group of people where you can share your deepest feelings and difficulties, people will feel comfortable challenging you if they think you are losing your bearings or getting off the track of your beliefs and values. Because they know your life story, they are able to perceive how prior events in your life or your personal needs may be influencing your decisions today.

YOUR PERSONAL GROWTH AND LEADERSHIP DEVELOPMENT

How will your True North Group help you grow as a human being and develop as a leader? An important part of your self-awareness is accepting yourself with all your strengths and weaknesses and having confidence that others will accept you for who you are. The confidence gained in your group enables you to face difficult situations in your life and work and to navigate them successfully.

On the other side of this coin, you learn in your group to accept others' differences rather than judging them. You gain the ability to celebrate their differences and to learn from people whose life experiences differ from yours. These experiences give you the capacity for sharing yourself in intimate ways and for experiencing high levels of openness with others. Your True North Group also serves as a support team when you are facing challenging times, just as you will develop the capacity for supporting others in their difficult hours.

In your True North Group, you learn how to give and receive feedback in nonjudgmental ways, without taking it personally. This is an invaluable skill that is essential to constructive human interactions, and it is a necessity for leaders who want to empower others to be constructive members of organizations meeting high performance standards.

Maureen Swan explains how her group impacted her leadership: "My group has enabled me to see where I am in my emotional development and how that enables me to be a better leader or disables my leadership," she says. "As a leader, I have learned that it can't be about me anymore. My role is to ignite people's passion around our common purpose."

CONCLUSION

As we have examined a variety of small groups that meet for different reasons, we have concluded that True North Groups are most effective in providing an environment of trust, confidentiality, intimacy, affirmation, support, and honest feedback. Your True North Group provides the atmosphere and the trust that enables you to grow as a human being and a leader across the full span of your life. Most important of all is learning through your group experience what matters most to you in life and how to stay focused on realizing it.

CHAPTER 3

Forming Your Group

BY NOW YOU ARE LIKELY INTERESTED IN FORMING YOUR own True North Group. This chapter provides you the details about how you should put your group together. Toward the end of the chapter we look at converting your existing group into a True North Group and creating your group in other settings — in your company, educational institution, or community organization, and even from remote locations.

Let's begin by examining a women's group that was formed eighteen years ago and has been together ever since.

FORMING YOUR GROUP

In 1992, Karen Radtke, a property management executive, met Jane Cavanaugh, shortly after Jane moved into the Wrigleyville neighborhood of Chicago. At the time, Cavanaugh was single and struggling to make a career in acting, while Radtke had been recently divorced. The two women formed an immediate bond that still exists today.

They talked about forming a group that would focus on their shared concerns. Radtke contacted five additional women, all of whom were strong, independent people who were successful in their professional lives. In those early years none of them had children and few had outside connections, so the group also became their primary social network.

All these women wanted a support group where they could talk about the pain of failed prior relationships and explore what was ahead in their lives. Radtke says, "We needed a place where we could lick our wounds. We also wanted to grow from sharing our lives, our dreams, and our spiritual journeys."

The group bonded quickly and provided each other with much needed support and encouragement. They decided to meet biweekly in one of the women's homes. Cavanaugh had natural talent as a leader, so she took that role with the new group. Radtke reflects on those days, noting, "Early in our group's life it seemed there were more tears than laughter. Over time, that was reversed as all of us supported each other in moving forward."

In those early years they read many of the same books and applied the main points to help them grow. The group members also had a common interest in social justice. For one of their programs they studied the life and work of an indigenous female hero in Guatemala, and then went to Guatemala as a group to examine this woman's work firsthand.

Radtke explains why the content of their discussions was so meaningful: "We studied much of the female literature that was beginning to explode in the 1990s." She adds,

> That led to discussion sessions on topics such as the worth of women, our strengths, how to discover and apply our talents, and the giftedness of our journeys. This group that started as a spiritual women's circle evolved into the sharing of our lives and supporting each other through myriad transitions.

Four years later, Cavanaugh brought the group a dilemma about whether she should move to Los Angeles to advance

EXHIBIT 4

Characteristics of Ideal Group Members

➤ Curiosity about themselves, others, and the world

➤ Willingness to challenge assumptions about life

➤ Comfort with self-reflection

➤ Commitment to continuing personal growth

➤ Respect for themselves and others

➤ Ability to listen without judgment

➤ Ability to hold confidences

➤ Willingness to be open and share their life stories

➤ Not self-absorbed

➤ Ability to commit time and energy to the group

ADDITIONAL CHARACTERISTICS OF IDEAL CANDIDATES

Sense of humor and positive outlook on life

Experience in small groups

Desire to be a good facilitator

---

her acting career. The other women strongly urged her to do so. As a result, the group was without its leader, so the remaining women converted to a member-led group. This transition was not an easy one because some members were less effective than others at leading the group.

Given this circumstance, Radtke decided she needed to take a stronger leadership role. She observes, "I tried to provide more leadership—maybe too much at times. I tried to change the purpose of the group to become more service oriented." She adds,

> Perhaps I failed to paint a grand enough vision. I felt we could continue to grow spiritually in a different way if we took our efforts out to the people. Some members of the group weren't ready for this shift and wanted to stay the way we were. I think groups should be about the tasks of loving, learning, and doing. This group was good at the first two areas.

Meanwhile, the women continued to support each other, especially when they had personal issues. In the past few years the group has become more social in meeting periodically for meals and celebrations. Cavanaugh and others who have moved away remain part of the group's broader circle and are invited to its events. Reflecting back on the past eighteen years, Radtke notes, "We are just as close as ever. This group has been a treasure in my life."

SELECTING MEMBERS FOR YOUR GROUP

The effectiveness of your True North Group depends on the quality of its members. In forming your new group, the most important thing you can do is to gather a group of people who are compatible and respectful of each other. As Peter Gillette notes, "The people either make or break your group." He adds,

> You can follow the ten commandments of leadership or the twelve commandments for small group formulation, but if you don't have the right people, the group isn't going to succeed. It is essential that each member

adds to the group's strength and diversity, rather than causing difficulties.

Solid members lead to better, deeper discussions of significant topics. They have the self-discipline and commitment to make time in their schedules for the group's sessions. They also attract other good members when the group wants to expand or needs to replace people who have left.

When forming a new group, it is essential to hold to rigorous standards and not to compromise. One or two ill-fitting members can easily reduce the feelings of trust and openness. This happened in an earlier group Bill participated in, when one member dominated each week with his son's issues but refused to look at his own role in the problems his son was having. Unless these issues are dealt with promptly, the damage to the group can be serious.

Agreement should be reached up front that True North Groups are not meant to be therapy or recovery groups. Prospective members with these needs should be directed elsewhere. For example, members in the early stages of recovery from addictions can benefit greatly from the appropriate twelve-step group, with support from their sponsor. Likewise, people in the early stages of grief will probably be better served in a grief support group until the pain has subsided.

Exhibit 4 indicates the characteristics of ideal group members. Someone who scores high in most characteristics will likely be an excellent member for your group. You can use this list, with modifications you deem appropriate, as a guide to assess your candidates. There may be other characteristics or criteria you want to add.

Just because some of your friends don't have all these characteristics doesn't make them poor candidates, but be careful about bringing in people who have low ratings on multiple "must have" characteristics. Considering that these people may become some of your closest friends, the time and effort you spend assuring the quality of the members will pay enormous dividends.

Having members who have worked in organizations and have been involved in community activities is also beneficial. They usually have dealt with ethical questions and have learned how to interact with others in ways that many solo performers have not. On the other hand, we have learned from experience that it is wise to avoid people who are self-centered or domineering, as well as those with poor listening skills who seem to "know it all." More difficult to deal with are well-meaning people who have perpetual issues that can drag down the entire group.

LOOKING BEYOND THE APPARENT: BEING OPEN AND INTIMATE

Beyond these characteristics lie many important qualities that are more difficult to assess but may determine the nature and character of the group. Jane Cavanaugh expresses it clearly when she says, "I want women who have depth, who are present, and whom I can trust—wise and deep women. When I tell them intimate things about myself, I need to feel confident that they are truly with me."

Retired human resources executive Paul Strickland observes about his group, "We want members who are solid and grounded in their values, but not any that are 'broken wings.' We want to spend time with people who are willing to discuss the deeper questions they are facing, rather than just looking for a quick fix."

Dr. Kathryn Williams adds, "You should avoid people who need a lot of attention, because they'll suck the air out of the group and the group won't be able to work on its real needs." She continues,

To determine if there is a good fit, it's important to

know what potential members are looking for and why they want to be in a group. Can they tell you more about their hopes and dreams than their problems? I ask prospects, "What do you still have to prove? Who do you admire and why? What's working well in your life?" Questions like these enable you to know the depth and breadth of potential members. You want people who are healthy enough to be open, to understand the importance of giving and receiving feedback, and to share deeply.

In reviewing the transcripts from our interviews, we were struck by the consistency of these comments and the evident passion behind them. Maureen Swan summarizes it well when she asks, "How has a potential new member reflected on things in their past?" She adds,

> She shouldn't expect life to be perfect, but she should appreciate life's paradoxes. She notices the nuances and gray areas of life. She should be comfortable with herself, expressing her weaknesses and acknowledging her difficulties.
>
> You don't want someone who tries to create an image for herself. Rather, she's reflective about life, has probably done some meditation, and is firmly committed to her development path. The reality is that none of us has life fully figured out. No one has ever reached a point of saying, "I'm there. I'm done now."

Frank Bennett, a hospital chaplain, observes about his group, "It helps to have people who are roughly the same age or in the same stage of life and who have had failures and disappointments and the depth that comes with these experiences." He continues,

This leads to a common level of understanding. Too broad an age range can lead to a disconnect between generations that gets in the way. Twenty years seems a workable age range, although I know of groups that work well which exceed that.

Eric Utne, founder of *Utne Reader*, says, "Prospective members should be interested in exploring the frontiers of the human spirit." Teacher Mike Seaman adds, "Individuals should have depth and willingness to be emotionally vulnerable. A high-functioning group must have open-minded members who aren't judgmental."

The most important thing for the group's success is that all its members enter the group with the assumption that everyone is trustworthy. This gets the group off to the right start in building relationships.

FORMING YOUR GROUP

Now you're ready to form your group. We suggest teaming up with one or two people whom you would like to have in the group and talking through what kind of group you would like to have and what each of you hopes to get from the group. Then draw up your list of characteristics of the kinds of people you would like to have and merge them into a consolidated list. After getting agreement on characteristics, each person should prepare a list of possible candidates. Who are the people you want to spend more time with in deep conversations? Compare notes with your colleagues and build a prospect list.

Starting with close friends is a natural move, as long as you realize that some tennis pals or book club friends may not be interested in the deeper explorations inherent in a True North Group. Often, friends in one context aren't involved in other parts of your life. Contractor David Scherf notes, "Our group started meeting because we are great friends. Being in the same profession enabled us to have a clearer understanding of the issues we face in our work lives."

The most desirable members may have busy lives and find it difficult to commit to a weekly session. Yet, as they experience the benefits, even the busiest people can find time in their lives if they are willing to reorganize their priorities. We suggest asking new members to try the group for a minimum of three months with no strings attached.

Issues in Forming Your Group

One of the most important issues in forming your group is the decision about whether you want a single-gender or a mixed-gender group. Our research has confirmed that both types of groups can work well, depending on what prospective members are looking for.

Organizational consultant Diane Nettifee observes, "Women have a unique way of being together and tend to be more open than men and more comfortable in talking about relationships." She explains,

> On the other hand, a mixed-gender group can build relationships with both men and women and have different kinds of conversations than an all-women's group will have. Often, it seems like mixed groups are speaking two different languages. It's a great benefit for me if I can stay open to hearing men describe their experiences and listen carefully to what they say, rather than translating it into my own language.

Dee Gaeddert, an executive in a large consulting organization, adds, "I like being in a mixed group. It's more reflective of the world in which we operate. I'm less interested in

talking about myself as a woman than who I am as a person."
Frank Bennett notes, "I didn't want to be in a single-gender
group because I like the balance of the energy between males
and females and the breadth of perspectives."

A related question is whether to have married or partner couples in the group. Among couples, it is relatively rare
to find equal levels of openness and willingness to share
deeply in front of their partners. On the other hand, we have
had a remarkably positive experience in our own couples
group, which has helped us learn about other couples' way of
addressing issues similar to the ones we are facing. Friendships that grow from couples groups can provide a lifelong
treasure, a result of getting to know other couples in a confidential yet supportive way—something that rarely happens
in our relationships with other pairs.

Other issues to consider are mixing ethnicity and national
origin. Bill's groups at Harvard mix ethnicity, national origin,
gender, religion, and sexual orientation but do not permit
couples or partners. Nevertheless, it is a good idea to discuss
these sensitive issues in advance, so these differences do not
develop into problems later on.

Your Group's Launch Meeting

From your initial organizing group, pick those who seem
to be most enthusiastic about a new group to become your
launch team. Review the list of prospective members and
agree on the list of people to be invited to the group's launch
meeting. Members of the launch team should be assigned
prospects to contact in order to ascertain their interest in
joining the group.

One matter to consider is the ultimate size of your group.
Through our research we learned that there are successful
groups with as few as four committed members and some
with more than twenty. In our experience, a group of six to

eight people works best. Four is too few if some are missing and may limit the variety of perspectives. More than ten members limits participation and airtime for everyone. We suggest at least five and not more than ten members to give your group a sufficient number for meaningful dialogue and adequate time for each member.

At the initial meeting, the launch team should explain the basic elements of the group, such as its purpose, the leadership model, the start-up curriculum, and the logistics of group meetings (see Resource 3). Suggested approaches for each of these areas can be found in the resource section. Resource 5 includes suggested meeting formats.

An effective way of bringing the group together for the first session is to schedule a half-day or full-day retreat. This longer time together enables the group to work through all the formation details and to review decisions about the group's makeup. It enables prospective members to discuss and reach agreement on the member contract (see Resource 4). Most importantly, the group members will have time to share their life stories, enabling people to get to know each other at a deeper level and to understand how well they fit together.

In the early stages it is not unusual for groups to experience fallout, as members decide whether they are prepared to commit the time and emotional energy the group requires. For that reason, you may want to start with a list of recruits that is double the desired size of the group. Or you can start with a small group and build it slowly over the first few months, adding people as needed.

GETTING STARTED: IMPORTANT TOPICS FOR FORMING YOUR GROUP

Now that your group has formed, the obvious question is, Where should we start? We recommend that your True

North Group begin by sharing your life stories, using the first four topics of the True North program described in Resource 1. In working with many successful groups, we have seen the powerful impact that sharing life stories has on building trust and openness in order to understand each other at a deeper level.

After agreeing on the contract in the first session, group members should talk about why they want to be a part of this group and what they hope to get out of it. In addition, they can share how they would like the group to help them in their personal growth and leadership development. Resource 6 suggests ground rules for group discussions.

The second session is an extremely important one as members share their life stories. Group members take turns telling the group about their lives, starting from their earliest years and working through to the present. Sharing these stories may take more time than is allotted for a single session, in which case sharing life stories can be extended into the next meeting.

For the next session the group's members go deeper into times they lost their way. The purpose of this session is to begin the examination of members' shadow sides and the ways they have succumbed or might succumb to seductions in the future.

The fourth session is potentially the most important the group will have. In this session people share the greatest crucible of their lives, describing the most challenging experience they have ever faced and what they learned from it. This session is important both to the person sharing and to the people on the listening end. Generally, people listen carefully to the person sharing, ask clarifying questions, and express empathy and support but are careful not to judge the person's experiences. In this session, in particular, it is extremely important that the norms in the member contract be observed.

Many people report that they discuss with this new group life experiences they have shared with few, if any, people in their lives. Others report seeing their crucibles in entirely new ways. This can lead to a healthy reframing of their most difficult experiences. Going into painful and difficult times and exploring one's dark side can be a cathartic and healing experience. In learning about crucibles others have faced, people realize they are not alone in facing great challenges. Done well, this session builds trust among group members and leads to higher levels of self-awareness and sensitivity to the challenges others face.

Equally important, members learn from these experiences what their passions and motivations are based on, and how they often guide the course of their lives. For example, one person who had a life-threatening illness during his teenage years saw himself as an overcomer. He then dedicated himself to helping other young people with life-threatening diseases. Another who lost her mother to breast cancer decided to pursue a career in medicine.

The member contract (see Resource 4) is crucial to making these four sessions work effectively. It provides the vehicle for having honest conversations in an atmosphere of trust and confidentiality.

LEADING YOUR TRUE NORTH GROUP

One of the most important decisions your group will make is about the model for leading your group. The leader is responsible for choosing the program, introducing it to the group, and facilitating the group's discussion. The facilitator also takes responsibility for the group's process, ensuring the discussion flows smoothly.

Our research and experience have shown that at least three leadership models can be successful: peer facilitators, professional facilitators, or a group member as permanent facilitator. Resource 7 provides a manual for facilitating True North Groups and a discussion of these options.

Peer Facilitators

In this model, the selection of discussion topics and facilitation of the group are shared equally by the members on a rotating basis. The peer facilitator model has the advantage of treating all members as equals and fully engaging them from the outset. This promotes involvement and commitment and provides opportunities for members to use their creativity and ideas to introduce topics. This is also the best model to enhance members' leadership by sharpening their facilitation skills and getting feedback and coaching from their peers about ways to improve their leadership.

Its disadvantage is that not all members have the same skills in facilitating the group or have interest in learning facilitation techniques. Peer-facilitated groups are also more likely to have difficulty dealing with conflicts between members and are less likely to sense when the group is getting off track.

In reflecting on the advantage of the peer-led groups, Peter Gillette drew a mental picture comparing peer-led groups to a circle and facilitator-led groups to a pyramid. He observes, "A circle suggests an equal amount of sharing. People have to go around the circle." Extending his metaphor, he says,

> When you're talking about a single leader, the group operates more like a pyramid, with the person who is leading at the top and the rest of the group below. Members of the group can hold back, waiting for the facilitator's opinion or guidance.

Commenting on his peer-led group, Ross Levin notes, "There is an absence of power. No one member has more influence or responsibility than any other." He adds,

> Because we have no titles and no ranking, you feel accepted as an equal. Therefore, it is easy to treat the others the same way. We have just enough structure to have predictable days we're going to meet, a location, and a member responsible to select the topic and facilitate the discussion.

Professional Facilitators

Historically, groups that discuss sensitive issues have used professional facilitators. The facilitator is charged with choosing topics, leading the discussion, and managing group process. Professional facilitators have extensive experience and proven skills in leading small groups. They can ensure a safe space for intimate discussions and can keep the group from falling back on intellectual discussions to avoid sensitive issues. The best professionals are well versed in sensing issues between members or in the group as a whole, usually well before the members are aware of the issues. They can draw out less verbal members and keep others from dominating the group.

The drawback to this approach is that it can be expensive and more difficult to organize. More significantly, it may create member dependence on the facilitator while lessening members' commitment and engagement. If the facilitators are not especially skilled, they may shape groups and discussions to their desires rather than to those of the members. Nevertheless, professionally led groups have proven to be effective for decades in myriad venues.

One variation on the professional facilitator is to engage a start-up facilitator for the first six to nine months of the group's existence, to organize the group, set up the initial process, and engage the group with outstanding programs during the early sessions. This can reduce the stress of getting the group off to a good start while preparing members to take over leadership after this initial period. The professional facilitator can be a role model for good leadership skills, which members learn from and can use when they take over leadership. This variation can work well, as it has for several groups that Doug has formed.

Permanent Facilitation by a Group Member

The third option is for one of the group's members to be the permanent facilitator for the group, at least for the first year or two as the group gets off the ground. This model is useful to get the group launched with solid continuity without having a stranger in the leadership role. This presumes that one member of the organizing group is skilled in facilitating groups and is willing to take on its leadership. Like the professional facilitator model, this approach can be applied for an initial period, after which the group shifts to a peer-led model.

Maureen Swan notes that having a member as permanent facilitator has worked well for her group. She explains,

> Our group has a leader responsible for content that prepares and sends out a reminder e-mail with questions to be discussed at our next session. Typically, she starts the session with a short reading, poem, or something for us to reflect on. Then she initiates the discussion and concludes with a brief check-in at the end.

Disagreements in Forming the Group

Doug had an unusual experience during the formation of one his True North Groups. His groups have applicants provide background and experience information in a brief biography that helps shape the interviews with prospective members. At the prelaunch meeting there were a dozen people invited by two business colleagues, and a few others who had earlier expressed interest in joining a group.

After the introductions, the group's purpose and methods of operating were explained and discussed. The ninety-minute meeting was pleasant, with great interest expressed in the model. It closed with the distribution of biographical forms. A professional facilitator was engaged to lead the group for the first six to nine months and to conduct interviews of prospective members.

Two weeks later, only a few biographies had been received. When queried, the leader of the business group said her friends and associates objected to the screening process and did not want to pay for the facilitator. As a result, Doug helped the business group get started as a member-led group, using the True North curriculum. The group seems to be meeting satisfactorily, but sporadically.

The four remaining people decided to pursue a True North Group separately from the others. They engaged a professional facilitator and invited a number of friends to join their group. They meet frequently and seem very satisfied. Following the start-up period, they shifted to a peer-led group.

No matter how well your launch session goes, there may be people who are unwilling to face difficult questions. Instead, they just decide to drop out. That's why it is important to follow up with everyone present to see if they are still committed to joining the group.

LOGISTICS FOR YOUR GROUP

Now you are ready to determine the logistics for your group—where you will meet, how frequently, the length of meetings, and whether food or beverages will be served. The choice of location is crucial. Ideally, it is private and quiet so that your group can engage in personal discussions without being interrupted or overheard by others in the vicinity. Workable locations include library meeting rooms, churches, some conference rooms where privacy can be guaranteed, family living rooms where interruptions can be minimized, and apartment building meeting rooms. It may take some moving around for the first few months to find a central place that works best.

Unless your group has a social purpose, most groups save time by avoiding serving anything but water, coffee, and tea during meetings. Restaurants and coffee shops should be avoided because it is difficult to keep servers from interrupting. Educator Mike Seaman shares the problem this caused his group, noting, "When we changed our location from one of our offices to a restaurant, the conversations became less intense and less personal. In a private setting, there are opportunities to let emotions be more exposed. In a public setting, openness doesn't happen as easily."

Maureen Swan talks about the importance of the right atmosphere. She observes, "Space is extremely important to the quality of a small group. You want a space that is warm and comforting, not a cavernous, cold space." She continues,

> For example, you don't want to meet in a large class-room. People observe the space and determine their own level of safety and comfort. If the group meets in a home, the hosts may feel they have to serve food, which can get in the way. Elements that induce social-izing also take time away from deeper discussions.

The next question to resolve is the frequency and length of your group meetings. We have learned that the most effective groups—those that build strong commitment and involvement—meet weekly or not less than every other week. Some groups feel their time only permits monthly meetings. This is workable, but it becomes more difficult if some members are absent at monthly meetings because they can lose touch with their group members. Once the meeting frequency is determined, it is almost impossible to increase it. Busy people can find time every week if they find the experience worthwhile. Aim for frequent meetings, even if it eliminates some members.

Diane Nettifee speaks from her extensive experience with growth groups, noting, "Commitment to the group is vital but difficult to obtain when you only meet monthly. When too much time lapses between meetings, it is easy to lose memories of the last meeting. Someone who misses a meeting will be away two months, which makes it even more difficult to maintain continuity."

Choosing a time and day of the week can also be tricky and requires flexibility. Many groups find it is easier to gather people in the morning, before work. Others find noon or late in the day works best. It may work best to put a stake in the ground and declare the time and date for the first few sessions, to see how well that works for the group.

Your True North Group meetings should last at least seventy-five minutes. This is the minimum amount of time required to get into depth about the issues raised and to give everyone an adequate amount of airtime. Many groups prefer to meet for one and a half to two hours to provide time for in-depth personal sharing. Several groups that meet only monthly take up to four hours for their meetings, to provide time for a check-in period as well as the program itself. In general, four hours or more per month is needed to develop the bonding and depth desired.

TRUE NORTH GROUPS IN OTHER SETTINGS

Thus far we have focused on how to form a True North Group with people in your community. Now let's look at other ways to create a True North Group. We begin by examining how to convert your existing group into a True North Group. Then we explore creating such a group in your organization, educational setting, and even when your members are geographically dispersed.

Turning Your Current Group into a True North Group

All the ideas on forming your group apply equally well to existing groups that want to transform themselves into a True North Group. This includes prayer groups, Bible study groups, grief groups, social groups, book groups, and a wide variety of other support groups.

There are hundreds of existing groups with the necessary ingredients to work together more closely in ways that enable all members of the group to grow. The True North Group model adds new dimensions to build on your group's foundation. The essential ingredient is having a cadre of members with good chemistry who seek deeper relationships and opportunities to explore life's important issues.

Many prayer groups and Bible study groups offer their members opportunities for examination of their religious beliefs and provide strong bonding around shared values. Evolving into a True North Group, or adopting many of the curriculum and process ideas in this book, can enable these religious-affinity groups to engage in a deeper exploration of personal issues and career challenges while retaining their commitment to religious exploration.

To make this transition work effectively, it is essential that your group agree on the member contract (Resource 4) and go through the first twelve topics of the start-up curriculum (Resource 1). This is most important, even if your group has been together for several years. First, you need to establish the norms of the group for more intimate, confidential discussions. Next, the topics of the start-up curriculum will bring out important things about each member that the group is unaware of. Finally, this process provides a strong bonding experience for your transformed group.

Review the process suggested in Chapter 7 on reforming your group before you begin the conversation with the people in your existing group. Think through the purpose of your revised group and determine what you need to bring it to fruition. This model can bring new substance and vitality to your current group. Not everyone in your original group may be interested in taking this new journey. Allow them to make that choice, rather than assuming they are not interested.

True North Groups within the Same Organization

Often peers who work together in the same organization or on task teams want to continue to meet on a more personal basis after the task is complete. They may be looking for people with whom they can share the leadership challenges they are facing and get honest feedback and advice in a confidential setting. In other cases, people in the same organization become friends and are looking for a group of people who will enable them to grow as individuals. For example, peer development groups might be beneficial to the following:

- Leaders from a variety of divisions and functions who need to achieve better alignment with other parts of the organization and become skilled in cross-functional interactions

- Existing task teams brought together for work such as acquisition integration, strategic analysis, major systems installation, or new product development and who want to continue to build their relationships

- Individuals who have high potential but have not yet been selected for an organization's upper-level leadership development programs
- Leaders who would benefit from developing comfort in dealing with people who have diverse life experiences

A large British company has employed the True North Groups model with its top one hundred executives in small sessions, utilizing professional coaches. This program is so successful that it is currently being expanded to its top five hundred leaders worldwide. Other companies have formed small groups of executive women to support their accelerated development. Such groups can be especially empowering to females in male-dominated organizations.

Community-Based True North Groups

In cities throughout the world there are sufficient numbers of interested people who have benefited from joining a True North Group. We have learned of groups consisting of

- Nonprofit and foundation executives
- Hospital administrators
- School superintendents, principals, or headmasters
- Church leaders
- Lawyers, physicians, or other professionals
- Club managers

True North Groups in Educational Settings

Bill's work at Harvard Business School has proven the value of this peer group experience for emerging leaders in educational settings. More than 1,800 people and three hundred groups have expressed unusually high levels of satisfaction with this process. True North Groups have worked effectively in a variety of other educational institutions, such as New York University and Georgia Tech.

These diverse groups of people, most of whom are meeting for the first time, immediately engage with their new peers in the exploration of their life stories, crucibles, and values. They are committed to working together to gain higher levels of self-awareness and self-acceptance. All of these groups use the peer facilitator model. Their ability to be open, confidential, reflective, and supportive as well as to provide astute feedback to their group members has exceeded everyone's expectations.

One graduate of the program says, "The groups are the most valuable vehicle for introspection I've ever encountered. I was more open with them than I've ever been with anyone in my life." Another notes, "This group was one of my best experiences in business school." She continues,

> It provided support, encouraged introspection, and consisted of the best and most intellectual discussions I've had. It gave me an opportunity to reflect on my life and share my feelings in an open and supportive environment. As a result, I faced things about myself I always knew were there but had tried to hide.[11]

This is applied leadership development at its finest. Through True North Groups, participants learn from people who frequently observe them in action and have no motivation other than making truthful observations. We recommend such groups for students in business, government, and international relations at both undergraduate and graduate levels. Participants in continuing and executive education programs are also excellent candidates, as are alumni groups.

True North Groups in Geographically Dispersed Areas

One of the great challenges many groups face after being together for a period of time is that their members are dispersed geographically yet yearn to stay together. This is especially true for Harvard's groups, when students complete their academic training and take positions in locations around the world. We have received extensive feedback from group members who have been successful in continuing their work together from remote locations, using telephone communications.

This raises the question of whether a group of people can *start* a True North Group from remote locations. The challenges of doing this are considerably greater than continuing an existing group that moves to different locales. However, modern electronic technology may be able to facilitate interactions like these, especially as multipoint video becomes attractive and cost-effective. Millions of people have experienced face-to-face video communications through a cost-effective system like Skype. Cisco Systems has developed a highly sophisticated system of this type for corporate meetings, called TelePresence, and a new system called ūmi that will be cost-effective for individuals.

These tools will make it possible for people to create True North Groups with members in remote locations. However, this process works considerably better if the participants come together for a weekend retreat to speed the assimilation and bonding process, and repeat these in-person experiences annually.

CONCLUSION

The first ninety days of your new group's life can be a real test. Just as moving into a new house has a shakeout period, so too do new groups. Finding, recruiting, and securing the right people are always the toughest and most important steps. Our suggested curriculum is designed to help you and your colleagues to bond quickly. The discussions it creates will help your colleagues open up and be willing to share personal issues that may be uncomfortable.

Decisions regarding frequency, timing, and location of your meetings can also cause some fallout, and the leadership model you choose will take some getting used to. It is important not to give up on this process. As your group settles into a positive groove, it will make all your efforts worthwhile.

CHAPTER 4

Norming

NEXT, WE EXAMINE THE PROCESS OF CREATING NORMS that enable your group to work together effectively and permit your members to achieve their goals. Norms include the rules, values, behaviors, work methods, and taboos that describe how a group functions.

Every group, family, marriage, and partnership has a set of norms. Some of these are explicit; others are unstated but detectable through observation and reflection. Not all of them are positive. Some poor behaviors in families, groups, and organizations can become normative and thus go unchallenged.

We believe it is important that your new group set explicit norms for how the group will operate. As your group decides questions of gender, meeting schedule and location, number of members, and mode of leadership, you are establishing the initial norms for your group. Some norms may change early in the group's life as the group either concurs with these initial ideas or proposes alternatives. As the group settles into a routine, more important norms will emerge.

Let's look at how one set of successful groups handles this process.

YOUNG PRESIDENTS' ORGANIZATION NORMS
MAKE THE FORUM GO

In our research, we discovered that the groups with the most explicit norms are created by the Forum of the Young Presidents' Organization. This is a global group of chief executive officers under fifty who run organizations with annual revenues greater than $5 million and more than forty employees. YPO chapters of up to one hundred members exist in most major cities in the United States and around the world. Members pay $7,000 to $10,000 annually to belong to YPO and to participate in its local, national, and international meetings. Presidents conclude their membership when they reach their fiftieth birthday, but many join an organization of YPO alumni so they can keep their relationships alive and continue to learn.

In the 1970s, some California members wanted to have a place and time to talk about personal and family issues, so they created the Forum, an intimate, confidential, and supportive set of groups that exist within most YPO chapters. The value of these groups is evidenced by the fact that 80 to 90 percent of YPO members participate in a Forum. Similar Forum groups have been formed for about 40 percent of YPO spouses, and additional ones have been created for the adult children of members. YPO members may remain in their Forum group past their fiftieth birthday, which provides a sense of history and continuity.

At monthly Forum meetings, members start by giving brief updates on their lives, which may lead to an initial discussion topic that evolves from issues shared by the members. The Forum facilitator, who is also a member of the group, keeps a "parking lot" of issues of interest that arose during prior meetings, when there was insufficient time to discuss them.

True North Group Norms

NORM	RATIONALE
Confidentiality	Essential for trust and openness
Openness	Exploring one's personal experiences
Trust	Without it, people won't share deeply
Differences	Respecting others' uniqueness
Listening	Active engagement with empathy
Judging others	Important to withhold personal opinions about others' beliefs
Feedback	Providing constructive suggestions
Attendance	Essential for group unity

Ron Kirscht shares why Forum groups have been so valuable to him and his fellow YPO members: "Leading an organization can be a lonely experience. There are decisions only you can make and responsibilities only you can fulfill." He continues,

> It is sometimes hard to confide in your coworkers or with friends in your immediate community about a challenge you're facing or a tough decision you have to make. That is even more the case in my personal life. My peers in our Forum group understand where I'm coming from because they face many of the same kinds of issues.

Several years ago, Kirscht faced a personal tragedy when his sister was murdered. His Forum group provided him a safe haven for sharing his feelings about this experience. He says, "It was too raw for me to have my coworkers and neighbors know much about this tragedy and how deeply I was affected." He continues,

> In my Forum group I could bare my soul. I talked about my fears, frustrations, and feelings, and knew I would be totally supported by the members of my group. I could share all the craziness that was inside me during this time. You can't run a company and talk like that with your employees. My group helped me think through my feelings and explore the pain. It was of great value in a situation I couldn't share at the office.

Forum groups have up to ten members. If the number falls to seven or fewer due to moves or resignations, new members are proposed by the YPO officer in charge of Forums. If the number falls to five, two small Forums may be merged.

These groups meet for four hours per month, with the location rotated among members' places of business each month. Typically, meetings begin with lunch on the same afternoon as the YPO chapter's dinner meeting. This represents a significant commitment of time on the part of busy presidents. Their continuing involvement is a clear indicator of the value of these groups.

Ron Kirscht elaborated on his group's benefits, saying, "These people act as my board of advisors. I bring them pending decisions and they point out my blind spots and flaws in the ideas. Usually, someone in the group who has had a similar experience will steer me in the right direction."

Kirscht describes one feedback process his group uses: "Meetings begin with each of us going around the circle saying out loud if we are 'good' with each of the other members. If I'm not, I have to bring the issue up at the outset with everyone there by telling the other member what the issue is. We don't try to fix the issue then. We just tell them, and that's the end of it."

Research conducted by YPO headquarters indicates that the Forum process has led to organization-wide norms. All Forum groups are led by a member facilitator who volunteers for a fixed period, normally one year. Forum members are trained in performing this role, and everyone is expected to accept this responsibility on a rotating basis. Members also undergo two days of training in group etiquette, effective listening, and meeting protocols.

Each member signs a confidentiality agreement and a conflict of interest statement, agreeing to avoid doing business with each other. Each Forum group may have additional rules and norms they have determined are necessary for their particular group, but the preferred mode is to avoid too much structure that inhibits comfort and satisfaction.

Privacy and confidentiality are crucial in the Forum. Some groups have a rule known by the code name Attila the Hun. If a member declares a topic to be Attila the Hun, it may never be brought up outside the group and may only be mentioned in a regular meeting by the originating member.

In screening potential members for his Forum group, Kim Culp says, "In order for the group to be valuable to you, you need committed partners." He adds,

> To get busy executives to commit to four hours a
> month plus two annual retreats, we need to be discern-
> ing about their level of commitment. When we add
> new members, we always add two at a time. Coming
> into an existing group can be a challenge, so we bring
> two so they don't feel like lone wolves. We prefer to
> have their first experience at a retreat, to provide extra

time to connect and get to know the others. Then they have ample time to share their stories and to learn the dos and don'ts of the group.

Both Culp and Kirscht have found their group experiences to be excellent learning opportunities. "I've received great insights into my personality," says Culp. He adds,

> The group holds a mirror up so you can see yourself as others do. You also realize you aren't the only one with your concerns and issues. Happiness has no connection to the balance sheet. We all have problems with our kids and our spouses. So you come to realize it is a more level playing field than you thought. I have received excellent insights about my style. These days I'm much less likely to have my anger flare than I was fifteen years ago.

Kirscht states, "The group has helped me keep little things from becoming big ones. I have a place to get things off the table before they build up and cause a mess. It has taught me to face into issues sooner than I used to, which eliminates that stress that comes from procrastinating."

DEVELOPING YOUR GROUP'S NORMS

Based on our own experiences with groups and research into other groups, we believe it is essential for groups to establish explicit norms at the time the group is formed. This matter is far too important to assume that positive norms will evolve implicitly over time. In the absence of explicit group ground rules, some members may assume certain norms are in place while others feel no need to observe them.

In Bill's MBA classes at Harvard Business School, group

members sign a member contract at the first official session. The contract is similar to the True North Group contract (Resource 4) and includes specific ground rules covering openness, trust, confidentiality, respect, tolerance, and feedback.

These explicit norms are closely interrelated. For example, before it is reasonable to expect group members to be open about highly personal matters, they must trust other members to treat as confidential (even from spouses) the issues discussed within the group. In this regard, Dr. Kathryn Williams observes, "All members should express their support of the confidentiality norm, as it seems to be the most crucial in predicting group survival. Without strict confidentiality, trust and bonding among group members will not happen."

Exhibit 5 summarizes why each of the seven norms is so important and how they are interrelated.

In the case of the Harvard Business School groups, we are unaware of any confidentiality breaches, which has been essential to their success. Students amaze themselves with how they can feel comfortable being so open. As one woman said, "I am sharing things in my group, with people I just met a few weeks ago, that I have never shared with anyone in my life, not even my parents."

We recommend that True North Groups develop their own contract in their first official meeting, with all members signing it as an indication of their commitment. By being explicit about the behaviors expected in interactions among group members, the group is much more likely to be able to sustain its success and delve deeply into the things that matter most to its members.

Architect John Cuningham comments on the importance of process norms: "We have developed a simple card, which I send out every January." He explains,

> The card includes meeting dates and the facilitator for each week, with names, phone numbers, e-mails, and

birth dates on the back. It helps to refer to the card and realize that you have the program in two weeks and have to prepare your topic for the group. We keep notepads at our meeting place to write responses to the questions and then compare our answers. This has enabled us to build up a rich collection of past programs and questions we explored.

BUILDING CHEMISTRY WITHIN YOUR GROUP

Having the right members is a necessary but not sufficient condition for a True North Group. It is equally important that group members develop a high level of mutual respect within the group.

Attorney David Dustrad talks about how his group was formed and why it is still together after twenty years. "We call our group of six 'the guys'," he says. "Our roots go back to our postcollege years." He explains,

> In forming the group, we recognized the need for connection to peers who could hold us accountable and with whom we could share struggles and challenges and celebrate the good things that were happening as well. What keeps us together is that we hold each other in such high regard. There isn't a guy in the group I don't look up to. We admire each other's leadership qualities and moral character, despite differences about current topics. There is a high level of moral integrity around the table.

For nonprofit executive Joe Cavanaugh, "In building the chemistry of your group, it is important that all your members adopt more subtle norms, like active listening, being present for others, demonstrating humility, and being mindful. You also have to bring yourself to the table—to participate and be appropriately vulnerable, sharing your warts and all. This is not work you can do by yourself."

Cavanaugh offers an interesting insight when he observes, "Most men I know don't need a small group to get charged up and ready for battle." He adds,

> Rather, they need a safe place to return from battle with their wounds—a place where they can be healed. I meet regularly with a group of guys that say, "If you fall flat on your face, come back, and we will be there for you."
>
> When I listen to my wife and female friends speak about their women's groups, it seems they have a different need. They look for other women to tell them, "Go into battle. You can do it." What they may need from their small group is courage and women who push them into battle and cheer them on when they succeed.

Venture capitalist Gary Smaby talks about how his group formed and developed bonds between members. He observes, "It's a completely personal choice as to whether one makes a commitment to participate." He continues,

> Initially, everyone was feeling the group out to make sure that the chemistry was right. We were all trying to determine whether it was worth the energy to join. Each of us was incredibly busy in our own realm. Eventually, we all reached the same conclusion. We were forming a unique group of peers. Every member offered a fresh, informed perspective, drawn from rich yet diverse experiences. And all had the capacity to lead. That's what enabled us to grow exponentially in the early stages.

On the other hand, businessman Jack Sell cautions, "Successful groups require mutual trust that can develop into respect and affection. People who are not respectful, not lifelong learners, or not open to learning from others won't be willing to stay in a group like this. In a sense, this becomes self-governing."

ADDITIONAL NORMS TO STRENGTHEN YOUR GROUP

Experience has shown that True North Groups are most effective when they operate as a peer group without any hierarchy. Having the members sit in a circle with no large table in the middle and no assigned seats is a good start. Avoiding titles is another. Although one of you has to be the organizer during the start-up phase, try hard to minimize this role as soon as possible.

We recommend that each group conduct an annual assessment (see Resource 8), followed by a discussion among group members. In part, this ensures that the norms in the member contract are reviewed, reinforced, and changed as needed. It also opens up the discussion about whether all members are getting the benefits they want. It provides an opportunity to address any norms that may be inhibiting member satisfaction.

Another useful norm is the adoption of regular retreats. In Chapter 3 we described the benefits of having a retreat for the first official group meeting. If that doesn't occur, then the group should hold a retreat within the first six months. Retreats are the fastest and best way for the group to bond and build trust. Overnight retreats are preferable, as group activities and the fun of preparing and sharing meals create opportunities for building relationships and breaking down barriers. Another option is to have a full one-day retreat in a quiet setting. See Resource 9 for additional ideas on retreats.

Once the group is formed and membership is stable, the group should develop a process for adding new members (see Resource 10). It is helpful to establish new member criteria that will be referenced by members when proposing some-one new.

New members can bring fresh ideas and experiences into a group that otherwise could become too predictable and too settled. Nevertheless, people are often concerned that new members may change the group's chemistry. As Karen Radtke notes, "Once groups bond, they become reluctant to add new members because they create changes and take time to integrate." She describes her group's approach:

> We put an empty chair in the circle that we keep open for the next new member. We believe it keeps the group alive and vital by filling that chair from time to time. When someone leaves the group, we have a norm to find a replacement and have only one empty chair.

John Curtiss, CEO of The Retreat, describes the process his group uses to add new members. "If we decide to add a new member, several of us will bring names to the meeting for discussion," he says.

> People who know the individuals offer comments, where these people are in their lives, and whether they are willing to share deeply. If we decide to proceed, we invite them to come and audit a couple of sessions. After that, the group decides whether they are a good fit or not.

Community volunteer Joyce McFarland notes, "We know that new members can change the dynamics of our group, so it is important for us to talk about them and meet them in person." She adds,

When new members are added, they talk about what they are looking for and we share about ourselves and how we each came to the group. This can be tricky business so we take time to do it well. Bringing in a new member can really be helpful in causing us to review how the group is doing and whether it is staying true to its purpose.

Early in your group's existence, you may want to discuss any concerns about previous relationships between members. These are to be expected, given the likelihood that your initial recruiting comes primarily from prior friends. It may also be helpful to discuss the destructive nature of cliques.

Frank Bennett advises that norms should be set about the kind of relationships that will be allowed between members. He asks, "Should a married couple be allowed in the group? What about a couple in a relationship? Should coworkers or relatives be in the same group? Are there any other relationships that might cause some members to feel uncomfortable?"

While it may seem rather formal to adopt so many norms at the outset of the group's life, experience has shown how important they are. Sound norms enable the group to explore important issues at a much deeper level and enable members to feel secure in opening up in the knowledge that everything will be treated confidentially.

We have learned the hard way that failing to reach agreement on how the group will operate can lead to many problems down the road. Misunderstandings between group members about expected behavior within the group may even cause the group to disband. We address those issues in Chapter 5.

Storming

HAVING ESTABLISHED THE NORMS NEEDED TO SUSTAIN
the group's vitality, we turn our attention to the other side of
the coin: behaviors that may impede your group, which we
call storming.

Because all of us are flawed human beings in our interactions with others, groups eventually experience a storming
phase. Yet many groups fail to acknowledge the difficulties
they are having. Denial is as alive and well in groups as it is
in families, marriages, and other social milieus. However, it
is much more constructive to address members' concerns in
a proactive manner.

New groups go through a honeymoon phase when things
are going smoothly and members are in harmony. Over time,
irritations at how the group operates or how some members
behave will inevitably grow. Storming kicks in when things are
not going well, when there is tension, or when some members
feel the group is not meeting their needs. Let's look at some
storming issues faced by one group and how it handled them.

ADDING NEW MEMBERS CAN CAUSE A GROUP TO DISBAND

Jane Cavanaugh was part of a group of professional women
that had been meeting for three years. The women in this
group shared deeply, the members participated fully, and no

one dominated the discussions. This led to high satisfaction among the members.

When two of the members left the group due to scheduling issues, the group decided to replace them. Two new women joined.

After six months, the different expectations of the new members became apparent. The original members looked to the group for discussions on topics that would enhance their personal growth and development. The new members were mostly looking for support in the personal issues they were facing. Cavanaugh notes, "It boiled down to we weren't on the same page about what the purpose of the group was."

The original members became increasingly dissatisfied. Two of them met with the facilitator to express their concerns and to share their dissatisfaction with what was happening at the meetings—how the focus of the group seemed to have changed.

"After trying to keep the group together," says Cavanaugh, "it became apparent that the different needs of the group were incompatible, and we disbanded."

Unfortunately, this experience is not unusual. Groups often wind up dissolving rather than resolving issues directly. In this case, many people got hurt. The original members lost a good thing in their lives. The new members lost their group without ever knowing why. And the facilitator lost her job. It would have been far better to force a resolution and accept the short-term pain in order to keep the original group together.

CHARACTERISTICS OF THE STORMING PHASE

How will your group know it has storming issues? Usually, one of the members picks up on someone else's complaints during or after a regular meeting. Talking behind someone's

EXHIBIT 6

Common Storming Problems

> Lack of member commitment

> Loss of trust among members

> Violations of the group's norms and values

> Absence of suitable boundaries

> Lack of openness and sharing

> Dogmatism or dominating behaviors

> Failure to move beyond intellectual discussions

> Inability to confront a problem member

> Breach of confidentiality

---

back is a common symptom. At first, it is useful to pursue these issues on a one-to-one basis to see whether they are serious issues or one of the members is merely letting off steam. Reaching some satisfaction of the matter off-line usually works best.

Some quick calls to other members will confirm or deny whether the issue is substantial enough to bring up at the next meeting. If the issues are shared by several people, then they need a full airing. Often, just talking the issues through is sufficient to avoid more significant actions, such as forcing members to leave the group.

Most storming events within groups tend to be short-lived. Either the group addresses its members' concerns and gets healthier or the group disbands, as Cavanaugh's group did. In our research, we did not find any group that stayed together through frequent, difficult storms.

CLASSIC STORMING ISSUES THAT BLOCK GROUP EFFECTIVENESS

Let's examine some of the most common issues that block group effectiveness and that can ultimately lead to the disbanding of groups (Exhibit 6). The stories that follow are true, although some have been disguised to protect confidentiality.

Lack of Member Commitment

One of the keys to making a group work is for everyone to observe group norms about attending all meetings and retreats, arriving on time, and staying until the meeting is over. If there are prework assignments, it is essential that they are completed in advance. Just one person who frequently misses meetings, perennially arrives late, or does not prepare in advance can destroy the harmony of the group.

As we discussed in Chapter 4, Young Presidents' Organization members are busy executives, yet the YPO Forum establishes clear norms regarding attendance, tardiness, and leaving early. Forum members strongly believe that meaningful discussions require full attendance. Hefty financial penalties are employed to reinforce these norms, and three absences in a year results in automatic expulsion.

Although these penalties may seem harsh for busy people, it is important for groups to reach clear agreement and to have operative rules about attendance issues. One such rule is that any member who must be absent e-mails everyone in advance to let them know. Likewise, if members need to leave early, they inform the others at the outset of the meeting so that their departure does not come as a surprise. Clear, enforced norms make the storming process less difficult.

Loss of Trust among Members

We know that trust is essential to making any group work effectively, but maintaining trust over an extended period of time is a challenge. Once lost, trust is hard to regain, as the following story illustrates.

A mixed-gender group of three women and three men had been meeting smoothly for about five years. At the first meeting of the fifth year, two members joyously announced to the group that they had been dating for several months. They wanted to tell the group as they were moving from a casual relationship to a more significant one. Since their relationship went against an explicit group norm, they decided to be forthcoming.

All but one person was supportive and did not feel the partnership would harm the group. The naysayer had issues with the female partner due to unresolved issues around a relationship she had with his good friend. As a result, he wasn't sure he could trust her again. This issue was not resolved until two meetings later, when the woman offered to resign if her new partner could remain. The group agreed and has survived the incident.

When trust is lost, it can sometimes be recaptured by people agreeing to meet to develop a workable solution, first in private and then with the support of the whole group. In difficult situations, it may be worthwhile to bring in a professional to mediate with the members. The goal is to reach a solution that everyone can support.

Violations of the Group's Norms and Values

What happens when one member violates the group's values? This creates a delicate situation that, if left unaddressed, can destroy the group's harmony, as in the following example.

A men's group that had been meeting for many years was surprised that one of its members had missed three consecutive meetings with no contact with anyone in the group. The person who originally sponsored him agreed to find out what was going on. At the next meeting, he reported the shocking news that this outstanding member of the community had stolen money from his clients, some of whom were close friends of the sponsor. The member was too embarrassed to face the group directly, so he asked the sponsor to sound out the others about his return.

When the group discussed the situation at its next meeting, people disagreed about what to do. Several people felt the only kind thing was to accept the member back, provided he acknowledged what he had done. The sponsor, on the other hand, was firm about the need to sever relations due to the member's unethical and illegal actions, which were revealed to go back for several years. In the end, the member was asked to leave the group. In spite of some hard feelings over the decision, the group eventually was restored.

Although the supportive nature of True North Groups emphasizes helping members through crises, some problems are simply too severe to keep the person in the group. In these cases it is better to ask the offending person to resign so that the remaining members can rebuild the group's harmony.

Absence of Suitable Boundaries

While True North Groups emphasize open sharing and intimacy, groups need to establish norms on just how far that openness should go. In our experience, this is especially true when sexual matters are concerned, as the following story illustrates.

A couples group that had been meeting for three years had to confront what several members felt was a boundary violation. One of the four couples chose to discuss their "open" marriage at a group meeting at their home. The man shared that he had had several sexual relationships with other women that his wife knew about. Subsequently, his wife decided to have an intimate relationship with a coworker who was several years younger.

This was simply too much for one of the women, who left the room and went into the kitchen. Another woman followed shortly thereafter. The two women talked openly about how uncomfortable they were with the discussion going on in the living room. Eventually, the entire group migrated into the kitchen. When the man who started the discussion appeared, one of the husbands lost his temper and accused him of using the term *open marriage* as a cover for his promiscuity. The group never recovered the closeness its members had experienced previously. Two years later, it disbanded when one couple moved out of town.

This example illustrates the importance of placing some reasonable limits on the subjects that groups talk about. It also demonstrates the importance of creating boundary conditions regarding the line between openness and excessive intimacy. These limits will differ from group to group, depending on the comfort level of its members around certain topics. The issue of sex is especially sensitive in mixed-gender and couples groups.

Lack of Openness and Sharing

On the other hand, a lack of openness also can cause a group to fall apart, especially if the group has agreed to share openly about personal matters. One of Bill's Harvard groups encountered precisely this problem. Five of the six members of the group shared their life stories and crucibles openly. When the group went around the circle, the sixth person always elected to pass rather than to share personally. Two of

the women got frustrated, feeling that this member was acting like a voyeur. They eventually left the group and decided
to meet on their own.

When Bill learned what was happening, he invited all six
students to his office. After the women described the situation, the man said that in his home country people rarely
shared openly. Bill noted that the member had signed the
members' contract committing to be open, and observed that
several other students from the same country had no trouble in sharing. The male student agreed to give it another try.
The group resumed meeting weekly with much greater success after talking through their differences, as the man finally
opened up.

This example illustrates the importance of all members
of a group being in agreement about how the group's discussions will proceed. If they fail to enforce that norm, the
group may disintegrate as its participants become increasingly frustrated.

Dogmatism or Dominating Behaviors

In order to have full participation and a balanced discussion,
it is essential not to let anyone dominate the discussion or be
dogmatic in their opinions. Having one person who dominates the discussion and refuses to listen or to respect different points of view can destroy a group.

Delia Seeberg, legal assistant in a law firm, describes a
stormy situation in her group. She says,

> After we had been meeting awhile, one of our mem-
> bers was more interested in taking the discussions in a
> direction the rest of us had no interest in. She was very
> forceful and at times refused to respect the opinions of
> other members. We finally decided to confront her,

suggesting that this group was not going to meet her needs. After she left the group, we returned to more balanced discussions among the remaining members.

Kim Culp shared a similar situation from his YPO Forum. He explains, "We have had dominant people that joined our group whom we had to ask to leave or help them understand their behavior was not appropriate."

In our experience, there is only one way to deal with people who are attempting to dominate a group: confront them and insist that they back off and let others talk more equally. Even if they agree, it is often difficult for domineering people to control their behavior. Thus, it is up to the facilitator to keep these people in check by asking them to hold back while other participants share their stories. This can be an important learning experience for a dominant personality.

Failure to Move beyond Intellectual Discussions

In small groups it is often easier to have intellectual discussions than it is for the group to discuss personal issues. If this is permitted to continue, people who are looking for personal growth will ultimately resign or simply drift away.

Bill had this experience in the first group he joined. One member in the group was extremely uncomfortable discussing anything personal, so he always took the discussion to the intellectual level. When his turn came, he frequently made jokes to cover his discomfort and then changed the subject. Although the group stayed together for several years, its discussions never went beyond the superficial.

It is important to gain agreement at a group's outset that its purpose is to share personal issues and that all prospective members must be willing to do so. In turn, this agreement must be enforced during group discussions.

Inability to Confront a Problem Member

One of the most common causes of groups disbanding is the inability of the group to confront a difficult member. If other people allow the problem member to dominate the group, this person ultimately could cause the group to fall apart.

A group of five women met weekly for more than twenty years. One of its members was going through a divorce and consistently dominated the discussion by ventilating her anger at her ex-husband and discussing the details of her new male relationships. As the divorce process got ugly, with charges and countercharges, she became more emotional and less willing to participate equally with the other women. The others tired of hearing her complaints every week and were frustrated that she didn't seem to take action to resolve the disputes.

The remaining four women met separately to talk about how to handle her. Rather than confront her or to attempt to find a solution that would keep the group together, they decided to disband the group. After two years apart, the four decided to regroup, bringing in a trained group leader. After the shift to a professional leader, however, the women felt less involved and less committed. When one of the four women withdrew, the group fell apart permanently, though they remain friends and see each other regularly.

A group that fails to quickly confront a problem member can put the group's future at risk. Dragging out a problem that is evident to all the members can erode the benefits for the remaining members and lead to its dissolution. It is a shame when a long-standing group cannot confront a difficult member and elects to disband instead.

Breach of Confidentiality

As we learn in the following story, nothing is worse than a breach of confidentiality. An all-women's group of professionals and executives had been meeting regularly for years. At one morning meeting the head of a large nonprofit shared her preliminary plans to join another nonprofit in the same city. Later that day, this member received a disturbing e-mail from an anonymous source claiming that another member of her group was sharing information about the potential position change. The nonprofit executive was mortified by the news and fearful that her board and staff might learn of her plans before she could tell her board chair.

After work, the executive and the supposed source of the breach met at a local hotel and discussed the rumor and the e-mail the executive had received. The other member denied sending the e-mail but acknowledged that she had told her husband right after the group's meeting. The executive was livid and told the member how upset she was about the breach of the group's confidentiality agreement.

Fortunately, the rumor did not spread. The executive was able to consummate the new employment agreement, inform her board chair and her staff, and begin plans for her departure. At the beginning of the group's next meeting, she described the entire story to the group and expressed displeasure with the gossiping member, who apologized profusely.

After three months had passed, the executive was still unable to forgive the other member. At their next meeting, she said that either the gossiper had to leave the group or she would resign. After a long and emotional discussion, a slim majority of the group agreed, and the misbehaving member had no choice but to resign. The atmosphere in the group remained chilly until the group took a weekend retreat, reached resolution, and agreed to put the issue behind it.

Trust is based on complete, not partial, confidentiality. Compromising the group's integrity can destroy the group. If people feel a breach has occurred, they must share their concerns, including the specific example. The group should then determine how to proceed. Only a clear and quick resolution can enable the group to heal and can renew the confidence the remaining members have in each other. The good news is that we are unaware of other confidentiality breaches.

OTHER POTENTIAL PROBLEMS AND POSSIBLE SOLUTIONS

There are some other storming issues that can occur in groups.

Members Feel Judged

Occasionally, members in a True North Group may feel judged by their peers when they share personal matters. In such cases, this issue should be addressed at the group's next meeting. Members having these feelings should have the opportunity to express their feelings and share examples. The group should then discuss how to give feedback in a constructive and nonjudgmental way. Resource 6 provides ground rules for group discussions.

Attendance and Timeliness

Poor attendance is a reflection of the members' commitment to the group, whereas timeliness is a matter of personal discipline. Assuming that attendance and timeliness are group norms, then appropriate discussion with a problem member should be had at a group meeting. If no standards exist, this issue could be a topic at the group's next retreat. If attendance continues to be an issue, it is best to ask the person to resign and to add someone with greater commitment.

Poor Chemistry May Create a Toxic Environment

As we discussed previously, negative chemistry between two members can be a divisive thing. Easy solutions are elusive, but it is essential to have the group work together to resolve the issue. This is so important that it should be a priority topic at an off-site retreat. Be prepared for the possibility that one or both of the members will resign.

If the conflicts are such that the issue cannot wait, then use a regular meeting to discuss and resolve the situation at the earliest time that everyone can be in attendance. Allowing this situation to continue puts the entire group at risk. Consider an outside resource if the situation cannot be resolved comfortably with members only.

REFLECTIONS ON STORMING WITHIN GROUPS

Storming is an inevitable occurrence in True North Groups. The key to the group's sustainability is not the avoidance of storms but the effective handling of them. Will the group face them directly and try to resolve them quickly, or will members refuse to face them and hope the problems will simply disappear? Will the group support those members who attempt to express legitimate concerns and force others to deal with them?

As we have seen in these examples, many seemingly healthy groups begin to implode when confronted with conflicts from within. Groups that ignore significant irritations do so at their peril. Without question, the quicker these matters are faced, the less tension will build up in the group, making a major blowup less likely.

One of the most constructive ways to avoid periodic storms is to schedule regular feedback sessions in which members go around the circle sharing their concerns and issues with the rest of the group. Often, the simple act of discussing these issues openly will clear the air. However, this may bring out into the open some long-smoldering issues that are more difficult to resolve.

Addressing storming issues and handling them effectively

is the mark of a healthy and high-functioning group. Now let's turn our attention to how high-performing True North Groups operate and sustain their meaning and effectiveness over a long period of time.

CHAPTER 6

Performing

NOW THAT YOUR GROUP HAS ESTABLISHED NORMS AND resolved its storms, it has earned its way into the performing stage. *Performing* is a term that describes a True North Group when it focuses on meaningful discussions and its members are in sync.

High-performing groups can sustain themselves for twenty years and more, but achieving this state takes committed members; thoughtful, ongoing programs; and adherence to group norms. When these conditions are present, there is generally a high level of satisfaction among the group's members.

A HIGH-PERFORMING GROUP

In November 1976, Ted Cushmore, a corporate executive, and Lynn Truesdell, a trial attorney, gathered for breakfast to discuss forming a group following the model of a spiritual weekend they had attended earlier that fall. The group's development began slowly as Cushmore and Truesdell each invited one friend to join the group. These first four members started meeting each week in a nearby restaurant.

The noise and lack of intimacy in the restaurant made their meetings difficult, so they moved to a nearby church. Although none of the members attended the church, its setting seemed more appropriate to the group's spiritual focus.

Lacking any specific membership or size objective, the group continued to add other friends until the group reached a dozen members. Meeting before work, they called themselves the Thursday Morning Group. After the group reached twelve members, only replacements were considered. In recent years, some members have retired to warmer climates, bringing the current size of the group to ten. The relocated members are welcome to attend when they are in town.

The group has met weekly for the past thirty-four years. Each member has responsibility to lead four programs per year. The group gathers for fifteen minutes of quiet time, and then the assigned leader for that meeting initiates the thirty-minute program. Typically, the discussion then shifts to broader topics of particular interest to the members.

Real estate developer Bruce Carlson explains, "We have evolved into a group that thinks about the world and its people and how our spiritual beliefs enter into our decision making. Often, we focus on the moral and ethical questions in all parts of life—business, politics, even baseball."

Looking back at the group's long existence, Cushmore believes the combination of the quality of the members and the nature of its examinations suggests "there is something bigger than us going on." After so many years together, life's joys and tragedies have left their mark on these men. In talking with them, it becomes clear that the sharing of these experiences has been enriching, enabling them to reflect more deeply on their own lives.

Ted Forbes, a retired executive, recalls with obvious appreciation how the group comforted and supported him during his wife's terminal illness. "In the early stages I needed to talk

EXHIBIT 7

Essential Ingredients for High-performing True North Groups

- ➤ Committed members who attend regularly
- ➤ Trust built upon confidentiality and cordiality
- ➤ Adhering to explicit norms
- ➤ Positive chemistry and bonding
- ➤ Sound facilitation of meetings
- ➤ Meaningful discussion topics
- ➤ Regular retreats
- ➤ Annual group assessment

---

about the mysterious nature of her disease and its effect on me." He adds,

> Without this group, I might have just buried and denied my feelings. The group also helped me clarify my new role with our kids. Shortly after Roxann died, I had a bad accident and needed back surgery. Once again, the group was there to support me. It was during these tragedies that the group has been especially meaningful for me, just as it has been for my colleagues who have suffered their own setbacks.

Because the group takes frequent ski trips in the United States and Europe, it has developed a reputation for great fun with terrific people. A membership challenge arose when nonmembers wanted to join the ski trips, but the group decided against including outsiders. Because the group includes a die-hard subgroup of baseball fanatics, it also developed some notoriety for frequent baseball excursions to new major league parks.

Included in the group are several highly verbal personalities who like airtime. On a weekend retreat to talk about making the experience even more valuable to its members, the group decided to introduce a metaphoric "talking stick." This Native American tradition reminds everyone that a person in the circle can only talk when they hold the talking stick.

According to retired attorney Norm Carpenter, "The concept of the talking stick has been a great asset. If you're 'holding the stick,' you get to finish your statement before somebody else jumps in. With so many ideas flying around the group, we needed a bit of discipline. It is not uncommon for a speaker who is interrupted to say, 'Hey, I still have the stick.'"

Reflecting on the group's discussions, Truesdell notes, "The longevity of the group and the relationships we enjoy have benefitted significantly from exploring our humanness and the whole human condition." He continues,

> Being human means sharing great joys and laughter as well as deep sorrow. Joy and sorrow are two sides of the same coin. Putting them together in a way that's healthy, whole, and enriching is difficult but crucial. This kind of personal interaction is vital, particularly for men, since we seem to have fewer opportunities for these kinds of conversations. Sharing such experiences and the attendant feelings, be they our own or those of others, is an important part of what life is about.

What has kept this group meeting weekly for so long? It not only has survived the test of time but also has been a meaningful part of the lives of its members. Looking deeper into their story, three things stand out:

- The members have developed strong bonds and a high level of mutual respect, trust, and caring for one another.
- Their programs provide substantive, personal, and worthwhile learning.
- The group has shared life's joys and sorrows and has supported individuals during difficult times.

The Thursday Morning Group illustrates the benefit of True North Groups in helping members grow and deal with great challenges, something all of us face eventually.

THE ESSENCE OF A TRUE NORTH GROUP

The heart of a True North Group lies in the substance of discussions that are designed to help individuals develop as human beings and leaders. Over the past seven years we have developed an in-depth program designed for individuals in True North Groups, which has been used by more than three hundred groups. The initial twelve-topic curriculum covered in Resource 1 is specifically designed to further personal growth and leadership development for group members. Equally important, it quickly promotes openness, sharing, and the building of appropriate intimacy within the group. This process closely follows the content of *True North*.

As outlined in Chapter 4, the process starts with individuals describing their interest in their personal and leadership development and sharing their life stories, including the greatest crucible of their lives. Covering these topics well may take more than one session per topic to ensure that everyone has adequate time to tell their stories and share their crucibles in sufficient depth. Sharing at such a deep level early in the group's existence requires careful adherence to group norms, especially confidentiality and nonjudgmental listening.

These sessions will likely result in a much closer bonding of the group as members have the opportunity to get to know their colleagues more intimately. In doing so, members gain appreciation for the life struggles other members have faced, which is not usually obvious on the surface. These discussions also provide other members with opportunities to reflect on how similar situations have affected their own lives. Stories like these are far more compelling than members' opinions about the economy, politics, or sports.

The next six topics deal specifically with the most important areas of one's development: self-awareness, values, passions and motivations, talents and capabilities, relationships and support teams, and living an integrated life. The final two topics in the twelve-part program address life's purpose and the empowerment of others. After completing the first twelve parts of the program, members of the group should give each other thoughtful and constructive feedback. Resource 11 has suggestions for giving and receiving feedback.

Following this initial curriculum, the group should develop a series of programs attuned to its interests. These can be selected by the group as a whole or by individual members in their role as facilitators. We recommend completing the start-up curriculum before turning to this list for program ideas. A list of suggested programs beyond the first twelve topics is provided in Resource 2. Further ideas and support may be obtained by contacting the True North Groups Institute, referred to at the end of the book.

Using this curriculum in a rigorous way helps group

members develop themselves, enables them to bond closely, and results in the formation of a high-performing group.

ESSENTIAL INGREDIENTS FOR HIGH-PERFORMING GROUPS

Let's explore the essential elements of high-performing groups. Exhibit 7 outlines eight key ingredients to ensure the group's longevity and ongoing value to its members.

Committed Members Who Attend Regularly

As Woody Allen says, "Eighty percent of success is showing up."[12] For a True North Group to sustain its effectiveness, its members need to commit to the group. Without this commitment, the group cannot survive. If prospective members are uncertain about their ability to attend meetings, it is better to face these issues early rather than letting them turn into storms later on, as the following story illustrates.

Ten prospective members for a mixed-gender group gathered in early 2010 in a large Midwestern city for their initial organizational meeting. As they began to make decisions about frequency and timing of meetings, the group started to thin. Two prospects left the group because they couldn't meet on Wednesdays. Another left because he was concerned the frequent meetings might negatively affect his work priorities. Another retired executive said she found the group's expectations of openness too threatening.

When the first session was held, three weeks later, only five people showed up. By the end of the session, two more people felt they couldn't make the commitment, so the group was down to three committed members. They set a norm requiring 80 percent minimum attendance or the member would be required to leave for a year. After careful screening, they recruited three additional members.

In retrospect, this group was fortunate to shake out

the partially committed people at the outset, rather than lowering expectations or being unclear about attendance requirements.

Trust Built upon Confidentiality and Cordiality

In the chapter on norming, we proposed that all members of the group sign the contract committing to the group's norms. In our experience, it isn't possible to expect members to be open and to develop trust unless everyone is committed to treat the discussions confidentially. People should enter into True North Groups with the assumption that they can trust each other, rather than assuming that other people have to prove themselves worthy of their trust.

Adhering to Explicit Norms

High-performing groups adhere closely to the norms agreed upon. They also observe the implicit, or unstated, norms of the group. That's one reason Forum of the Young Presidents' Organization groups have been so effective and have expanded so rapidly. Less-effective groups tend to have much lower compliance with their norms, which may cause them to dissolve.

The challenge comes when norms are violated. How the group goes about confronting these issues will determine its effectiveness in meeting the needs of its members over the long term. Here's an example of how our group dealt with a growing attendance problem.

Our group originally met on Friday mornings, which worked well for many years. Then it became noticeable that attendance was slipping. Discussing the issue at a meeting, it came out that several members who had acquired lake cabins were going to the office early on Fridays so they could leave town at noon to beat the traffic heading north. As a result, the group agreed to try meeting on Wednesdays. Strong attendance returned, and the meeting date has held ever since.

Discovering that an old norm is no longer working and addressing it quickly is an excellent way to keep member satisfaction high.

Positive Chemistry and Bonding

At the heart of any successful group that has staying power are the bonds that develop between its members and the positive chemistry within the group itself. As elusive as chemistry is, its importance rises when the group encounters problems within the group. If positive feelings and trust exist among the members, they will tend to address problems and resolve them. If these factors are not present, the group is much more at risk.

The importance of bonding and chemistry also impacts the group's discussions. Do the members genuinely respect the differences among their points of view? Are they willing to express their differences without rancor or confrontation?

As Gary Smaby observes about his group, "You need free exchange—both positive and negative—about what's working, in order to find out how you want to proceed." He adds,

> This group has had enough power to dynamically redirect any discussion if it's veering off in the wrong direction. There's no hierarchy here. By consensus someone may be asked to lead the group for several sessions, but it is still a flat organization. Over time, all of us share the leadership role.

We have found that interaction between meetings also can help build bonds. So can group retreats where everyone has the chance to participate in group activities and the group can engage in more extended discussions than is possible in a time-constrained meeting format.

Sound Facilitation of Meetings

In Chapter 3 we discussed the various types of leadership that your group can use—peer facilitators, professional facilitators, or group member as permanent facilitator. Regardless of the type of leadership model chosen, it is important that leaders do their job well in facilitating the group and staying attuned to its needs.

The quality and variety of facilitation are important to keeping meetings interesting and ensuring that participants are engaged. Having rotating peer facilitators helps keep the meetings fresh with a variety of styles. Staying with one facilitator for too long can also make the group too dependent and less engaged.

When members rotate leadership, there is a healthy expectation that the quality of the discussions you lead must be up to the group's standards. If some members need coaching to improve their facilitating skills, feedback from others can help, or they can refer to the facilitator's guide in Resource 7 for ideas about leading the group.

Meaningful Discussion Topics

Earlier in this chapter, we discussed the kinds of discussion topics that generally will make your True North Group meaningful to its members. The key is to choose topics that engage participants at a personal level. If discussions become intellectual, there will be a tendency to avoid feelings and to stay away from personal experiences and beliefs. If this happens, the group will devolve into a think tank with its members just exchanging knowledge. This can be interesting, but it doesn't lead to personal growth and leadership development. Here's an example of this kind of situation.

A mixed-gender group that had been together for two years was conducting its member survey at a retreat when Jennifer, its youngest member, asked for help. She had received feedback that the programs she led in the past year were less than stimulating. Jennifer had chosen topics from the newspaper about unsettling situations around the world.

As a supervisor in a retail organization, Jennifer had limited experience with leading groups, either in the workplace or in the community. A psychologist offered to coach Jennifer on facilitating her group. His advice was to choose topics that caused members to reflect on their experiences and their beliefs. As the psychologist's advice shows, choosing programs that cause people to reflect on their lives rather than asking for their opinions is the best way to engage the group in meaningful discussions.

Regular Retreats

Our research indicates that the experiences people remember and most cherish come from group retreats. Retreats can be held anywhere apart from the group's regular meeting place. The best ones usually involve being out in nature, away from the city, at someone's cabin, a retreat center, or a bed-and-breakfast. The availability of group activities such as hiking, biking, skiing, or volleyball enhances the experience. This kind of retreat setting lets people loosen up and get to know each other better. Resource 9 provides more suggestions for retreats.

A retreat is a perfect time to explore a big topic that requires more time for prework, reflection, and discussion. For example, a three-part question can work well, such as, What are you doing to develop yourself in body, mind, and spirit? After asking participants to do prework on the question, retreat discussions could be held in three separate sessions, with time at the end or in a fourth session to examine the interrelationship among these three aspects of oneself.

An off-site retreat is also a perfect time to explore how the group is doing from a process point of view. The group may want to review its norms, do a feedback exercise, renew the member contract, or discuss whether to expand the group. To ensure the unity of the group, it is important that all members be present for these events.

Annual Group Assessment

Relationships in True North Groups require attention to maintain a high level of satisfaction. Being able to tweak the operation from time to time keeps the group meetings sharp and meaningful. It helps to have one of your group members watch for potential storm clouds within the group.

Even the best-functioning groups need some corrections to keep the edge sharp. Keeping track of member satisfaction through an annual group assessment can head off potentially bigger issues ahead. It is beneficial to take the pulse of the group once a year, using the member satisfaction survey (Resource 8).

Here's an example of a group that made effective use of an annual assessment. A group of seven women called themselves Mick's Chicks, due to the predominance of Irish ancestry. The women got along well but tended to focus more on social discussions and sharing meals than on substantive issues. In its first year, Diane hosted an overnight at her nearby vacation home. This retreat was so successful that the group decided to meet there every April.

In the third year, the group conducted its first group assessment, which lasted nearly the entire afternoon. As a result, the group decided to revamp its regular discussions, to move away from the superficial and focus on more personal matters. They also agreed to take the pulse of the group every April.

REFLECTIONS ON HIGH-PERFORMING GROUPS

One danger of a high-performing group is taking the group's work for granted. It is easy to get complacent when the group is doing well, especially during the early years, when you need to keep refining the group's practices to maintain high member satisfaction. In groups with the highest commitment and member satisfaction, it is usually the relationships among the members and their willingness to engage in probing discussions that rate as the most important factors in satisfaction.

Gary Smaby observes of his high-performing group, "I don't think the topics we discuss are as relevant as the discussion that flows from them." He adds,

> What's valuable about the discussion is not so much
> where it starts but how it evolves. The initial question
> is often forgotten because someone will take the
> discussion in a new and interesting direction. It's not at
> all uncommon for us to veer from the original topic
> proposed by the facilitator.

Several groups have raised the question of whether the group's purpose should be expanded beyond its members' personal development to include an overarching community goal. There are groups that do joint service projects like Habitat for Humanity or helping people in Haiti. Others bring their families together at seasonal times to sing for shut-ins. Some address issues like early childhood education. In the end, most groups decide to let their members pick their own issues and organizations to support, so the group can focus on its own development.

The satisfaction that develops from being part of a high-performing group is enormous, but the group must constantly renew itself. The steps recommended throughout these chapters are essential to developing your True North Group and keeping it on track as a high-performing group.

CHAPTER 7

Reforming Your Group

THERE IS A TIME IN THE LIFE OF EVERY GROUP WHEN
it faces such major issues that a significant restructuring of
the group is required, as fine-tuning is unlikely to address
the issues. Instead, the group needs to step back to reexam-
ine itself and determine how its purpose and structure need
to be changed. This deeper look can be accomplished at an
off-site retreat. Here's the story of a group that went through
not just one but two such restructurings.

A GROUP EXPERIENCING A DOUBLE REFORMING

The group began uneventfully in 2004 as a mixed-gender
group of four men and three women. Doug was the professional facilitator and Craig Neal played an important role in
gathering new members. For the first three months attendance was strong, participation was excellent, and all members seemed pleased with their new colleagues.

Suddenly, the group started to fall apart. Two people had
serious family matters that forced them to resign. A third
person encountered a business crisis that caused her to drop
out. Another woman disappeared with no further contact
and did not respond to phone calls or e-mail messages.

Within three weeks the group was down to just three people. This was too small a base upon which to build a vital group, but all three stayed with the program and provided a solid core. Recognizing that the group had to be reformed, Craig and Doug reviewed what had happened, to determine if there was anything foreseeable in the backgrounds of those who had left. Nothing turned up, as three of the four had sudden life issues that were unpredictable. All of them later joined other groups.

Nevertheless, the remaining members agreed to screen new prospects more carefully to see if they had any noticeable issues or concerns. They put together a list of people who would be good additions to the group. The target was to add five new members.

A list of eight prospects yielded three women and five men. The first five who accepted invitations to join happened to be male. Two of them had never been in a group before, yet they lasted long past the group's two-meeting trial. One of them, Ross Levin, talks about his experience: "Although I am a nonjoiner, I admired the people who were forming the group, so I decided to give it a try." He adds,

> I stay because I get a lot out of the group and really like the people. We talk about interesting issues in a way that doesn't happen in my daily life. All these people want to make a difference in the world. Our commitment comes from who we are and how we connect. Bonding is crucial to building a group that has some stickiness.

Gary Smaby observes, "Everyone was feeling out the idea, to be sure the chemistry was right and it was worth the energy to form and sustain the group." He goes on,

EXHIBIT 8

Common Reasons for Reforming a
True North Group

> New blood is needed to reenergize the group

> Members want to change the group's purpose or
  character

> Several people depart simultaneously

> The group splits into two smaller groups

> Trust is broken

Each person brings something unique, and that's what
makes it exciting. In the early days of our formation it
enabled us to grow exponentially. To maintain the
group's commitment, we need to have a free and open
exchange about what's working and what's not. My
personal growth has come from exposing myself to
different points of view and not being rigid and dogmatic in my responses. We come from different life
experiences, but together represent a unique combination of intellectual, emotional, and spiritual energy.

Two years later one of the initial members acknowledged he
had an addiction problem that forced him to withdraw from
the group. The remaining members considered replacing him
but decided to stay with the current lineup. After a year, he
applied for reentry, but the group felt he had not recovered
sufficiently.

At the group's retreat the following spring, Doug withdrew as facilitator, and the group's second reforming phase began. The group decided to shift from a professional facilitator to rotating responsibility for leading the group's monthly sessions to each of the members. Meeting times were also lengthened.

An important decision was made to double the number of annual retreats. Volunteers signed up for program ideas for the retreats as well as meal responsibility and transportation. Long walks in the woods near three cabins used by the group were a highlight.

The changes clearly reflect a shift in how the group operates and how it perceives itself. Based on members' feedback, commitment to the group seems stronger since the changes. At this point, membership remains at eight, with no interest in expanding.

WHEN IT IS NECESSARY TO REFORM YOUR GROUP

Reforming your group goes well beyond incremental changes. Quite often, the thoughtfulness of going through a reforming process and the commitment of the members that results from it will determine whether your group can renew itself and remain vital. Don't expect that all the members of your group will greet this idea with enthusiasm; it is likely that several of them will resist or resent proposed changes.

After you have been a part of a group for several years, it is normal to feel comfortable with the status quo and be reluctant to make significant changes. Inevitably, some members will want to keep the group the way it is, in spite of flaws in its process, and may feel threatened by a discussion of reforming.

Some common signals that trigger a reforming process are shown in Exhibit 8.

New Blood Is Needed to Reenergize the Group

Even the best groups can become complacent. At this point, the members need some spark to breathe new spirit into the group. The first step is for members to discuss their feelings and then propose possible solutions.

If the group is unsuccessful in stimulating new energy and enthusiasm, it may be time to add some new members. New faces with vibrant energy, often drawn from a younger generation, are a tonic that can be helpful in challenging some of the group's norms, especially those that have developed implicitly rather than explicitly.

Members Want to Change the Group's Purpose or Character

Some groups may want to convert from a book club or a prayer circle to a True North Group; however, this may not please all the members. These dramatic shifts call for careful consideration to keep the group from imploding. An outside facilitator often can be helpful in guiding this process.

Several People Depart Simultaneously

Any change in membership will change the culture of the group. When members are lost, remaining members need to take time to reflect on what has happened and decide what steps, if any, they want to take to replace departed members.

Additional members should not be considered until the group takes an honest look at itself and understands the satisfaction level of its remaining members. It needs to understand the environment into which it is inviting replacements. It is often hard for groups to see themselves as others see them.

If members left because they were dissatisfied with the group, there is the added sting of rejection. It is important for someone in the group who is close to these members to meet with them individually to determine their real reasons for leaving. Then, the remaining members should have an honest discussion about the feedback and consider changes in how the group operates, in order to respond to the concerns raised. If this is not done, the group may find that additional members also depart.

The Group Splits into Two Smaller Groups

Sometimes groups experience too much of a good thing. This occurs when so many new people join a group that it becomes too large. People may feel they are not getting enough time to share their issues and opinions. In this case the group should consider dividing. Having experienced such a split thirty years ago, we learned how important it is for the group's strongest leaders to be divided among the two groups so that both groups feel balanced.

If a group decides to split due to differences about what its members want to discuss, how open they will be, or conflicts regarding scheduling or meeting location, each of the split groups should be treated like a new group and go through the first-year curriculum again (see Resource 1). In particular, new groups should revisit the member contract, determine new norms, and share their life stories and crucibles once again. In this way, all the members will be on the same footing, in spite of differences in longevity in the prior group. These steps will do a great deal to ensure that everyone feels equal in the new group.

Trust Is Broken

A significant loss of trust is the most difficult issue to repair, as there are no easy methods to regain trust. It is hard work to recapture the spirit within the group. In these cases, having an off-site retreat or bringing in an outside resource may be essential to providing a safe harbor.

Typically, trust cannot be rebuilt until all members have had a full opportunity to express their feelings about what has happened. Then the participants, led by the facilitator, need to develop a healing process or even a ceremony to reunite the group. Generally, healing can be accomplished most effectively at a retreat, away from the pressures of regular group meetings.

A PROCESS FOR REFORMING YOUR GROUP

When a group recognizes it needs to undertake a reforming process, the first step is to survey the members, either orally or in writing, to see how committed they are to rebuilding the group. Next, the group should diagnose the group's issues and determine the greatest challenges it faces. Once they have a good handle on these conditions, members can develop a plan to restore the group's health.

Early in this process you need to determine whether the group needs to change its purpose. A review of the norms the group has followed can provide some clues to improvements in this area. Then, the number and characteristics of new members to be added should be discussed. On the other hand, it makes no sense to bring in newcomers unless the group has resolved its issues.

Not surprisingly, many groups make only cosmetic changes when more significant changes are needed. This trap can be avoided by being tough-minded and not settling for changes that do not deal sufficiently with the root causes of the group's ineffectiveness.

WHEN IT IS TIME TO DISBAND

There is a time in the life of every group when it needs to disband. There is no standard length of time a group should stay together. A successful group can last as few as three years or as long as fifty years. Rather than by longevity, think of measuring the strength of the group by the bonds that develop between members.

How will you know it is time to disband? Although there are no fixed rules, here are some signs that may suggest dissolution should be considered:

- A reforming effort has not changed member behavior regarding attendance and quality of discussions.
- Member resignations continue, and the group has difficulty agreeing on new members.
- Member dissatisfaction continues for more than a year.

To mark the ending of the group, it is wise to have a formal process or ceremony to conclude the group's time together. Even if the group disbands, some of its members may choose to start a new group. If so, we recommend a cooling-off period of three months or more before meeting to reorganize. This will clear the air and weed out less-committed members.

REFLECTIONS ON REFORMING GROUPS

Rather than viewing the need to reform the group as a disappointment or a failure of the group itself, it is healthier to look at it as an opportunity to build a more effective group that can play a more important role in the lives of its members. Just as all large organizations reach the time when they need to transform themselves, so too do True North Groups. If the reforming process is done well, the group will emerge stronger and more unified afterward. That makes it worthwhile to go through a rigorous and often painful process of transformation every few years.

Why Your True North Group
Is Important in Your Life

IN PREPARING TO WRITE *True North Groups,* WE HEARD many interesting and powerful stories from people about the impactful experiences they have had in their small groups and the profound impact these groups have had on their lives. In reflecting upon our personal experiences in and with groups, we believe forming a True North Group will be one of the most important steps you take in your life. Your group can do so much to help you grow as a human being and become a more effective, more empowering leader.

In a world where the difficulties we face every day often feel overwhelming, your group will provide a powerful link between your personal life and the organizations in which you participate. It will enable you to stay grounded and build stronger relationships at work, at home, and in your community.

If your group sustains itself for a number of years, you will find that its members become some of your best friends. Together you have the benefit of being part of each other's lives and sharing your life histories. You will be bonded by the joys and sorrows you have shared together. Having this history enables you to connect on a much deeper level.

The time is ripe for a rapid expansion of True North

Groups to fill the void so many people feel as a result of not having opportunities to share themselves, their lives, and their stories in intimate, confidential settings. By providing a supportive place for deep discussions about life's most challenging questions, True North Groups enable us to become fully human and fully alive, awakening to the enormous possibilities within each of us to make a difference in the world through our leadership.

More broadly, the spread of True North Groups can become a small but important step toward healing modern society, with its multiplicity of ills. We believe the collective power of small groups can contribute to the creation of a healthy fabric for people to live lives that enable them to realize their dreams, find purpose and meaning in their lives, and build healthy communities.

May your group experiences be as rewarding as ours have been!

RESOURCE I

Start-Up Curriculum (First Twelve Topics)

RESOURCE 2

Additional Program Ideas

RESOURCE 3

The Group's Initial Meeting

RESOURCE 4

Member Contract

RESOURCE 5

Meeting Formats

RESOURCE 6

Ground Rules for Group Discussions

RESOURCE 7

Guide for Facilitating Groups

RESOURCE 8

Member Satisfaction Survey

RESOURCE 9

Group Retreats

RESOURCE 10

Adding New Members to Existing Groups

RESOURCE 11

Giving and Receiving Feedback

RESOURCE 12

Research Process

Start-Up Curriculum
(First Twelve Topics)

EARLY IN THE LIFE OF A TRUE NORTH GROUP, IT IS especially important to be open, in order to initiate intimacy. This helps develop a bond between members who realize they share many of the same longings and life experiences. From these new relationships comes a measure of trust that members can be vulnerable and share their life issues among new friends who will handle them with care and concern.

The facilitator for the first session should send out the questions outlined in this chapter. Doing so before the meetings enables members to prepare in advance and provides more time during each meeting for discussion.

Coming early in the group's life, these personal questions will help shift the discussions from the intellect to the heart. As a well-known anonymous quote says, "The longest journey you will ever take is the eighteen inches from your head to your heart." This is where real openness begins, enabling participants to overcome feelings and personal experiences hidden behind the shield of fear. These initial exercises are designed to start the process of reflection and sharing.

Each person needs a notebook in which to respond to these questions. The notebooks will provide participants with a valuable look at themselves, the challenges they have faced, their private observations, and useful inputs from other members of the group.

TOPIC 1: EARLY LIFE EXPERIENCES

At the end of the agenda for the launch meeting (if there is time) or at the start of the next meeting, the following exercise introduces the suggested curriculum for the first twelve topics. This first exercise helps the other members get to know you in a deeper and more intimate way. Use these questions to guide your sharing.

1. What people or events have had the greatest impact in shaping your life?
2. Describe your relationship with each of your parents, both good and bad.
3. What impact have your parents had on your life?
4. What relationships with siblings, other family members, mentors, coaches, and teachers have most influenced you? In what ways?
5. What are the experiences, both positive and negative, that had a major impact on you and your life?
6. What are the principles that guide your life?

Allow fifteen to twenty minutes for each person to provide responses to these questions. If all group members do not have adequate time to answer the questions, the discussion can be carried over into the next session. This same notion applies to all twelve topics in the start-up curriculum.

TOPIC 2: YOUR LIFE STORY

Share your life story with the group. Highlight the major events in your life, starting with your birth through today. Include highlights, low points, transitions, and critical events. Add key people, important teams or groups, important places, and vital experiences that have shaped and impacted you in an important manner. You may want to create a diagram to depict the events in your life as ups and downs. Or you could use the Path of Life exercise found in *Finding Your True North: A Personal Guide.*

As new members are added to the group, they should be asked to complete these first two topics during their first two sessions with the group. In this way, everyone has a shared understanding of each other's life histories and their stories.

TOPIC 3: HOW PEOPLE LOSE THEIR WAY

Rare is the life path that has no detours or missed turns en route to satisfaction and achievement. Some of these wrong turns are caused by life's misfortunes. Others are self-induced. In any case, there are usually corrections we can make to return to our intended journey, even though we may have to make some alterations in plans or goals. The key is to persevere in the journey and to maintain the flexibility to adapt as needed.

While telling your life story, you recounted events, achievements, misfortunes, and victories. Some yield to the pressures they are under and deviate from their values, beliefs, and convictions. Others get sidetracked and seduced by the rewards of money, fame, power, or the recognition of their peers and bosses. It is almost impossible to go through life without getting off the track of your True North at some point. The important thing is to recognize what is happening to you and what is motivating you at a deeper level, and to listen to feedback from those around you.

This exercise concerns six situations that you and your fellow members can study to see how each might have contributed to some of your missteps. This will help you learn how to reduce their occurrence in the future.

1. Describe a time when you succumbed to pressures and temptations and deviated from your core values.

2. Can you recall a time when you behaved like an imposter? What led you to act that way?

3. When did you feel you were weighed down by obligations, work, and problems? How did you respond? What would you do differently if you could do it over again?

4. Describe a situation in which you let yourself be seduced by money, fame, or power. What happened? What was the result?

5. Share a time when you rationalized a failure.

6. Describe a time when you failed to ask for help from mentors or guides.

TOPIC 4: THE GREATEST CRUCIBLE OF YOUR LIFE

What has been the greatest crucible of your life — that singular experience that has tested you to the limits and impacted your life? Crucibles can be painful personal or family events, something in your work, events in your spiritual journey, or the death of a loved one.

1. What was this experience like for you? What were you feeling at the time?

2. Describe how your life changed as a result of this experience. You may have had more than one such event, but for this purpose, choose the one with the greatest impact on your life.

3. As you look back on this experience, how do you see it today? In what ways has it had a negative impact on you? What might be the positive aspects of this experience and the ways in which you changed as a result?

Be sure to allow adequate time for each individual to describe his or her crucible in as much detail as they choose, and for group members to listen actively and with empathy, without judging the individual experiences.

TOPIC 5: SELF-AWARENESS

An essential element in our leadership effectiveness and satisfaction in life is self-awareness. One of the hardest things to do in life is to see ourselves as others see us. Only through self-awareness can we understand ourselves and perceive our impact on others.

With self-awareness, we begin to have compassion for ourselves and for what we have experienced and overcome in our lives. It is only then that we can begin to accept ourselves as we are.

Your True North Group gives you the opportunity to accelerate self-awareness in ways that are difficult to do on your own. Peer feedback in a trusting environment is invaluable in the process. Working with your True North Group will accelerate your knowledge of the impact you have on others, through the feedback you receive from them.

Begin by answering these questions and then sharing your answers with the group:

1. Describe a situation in which you demonstrated a lack of self-awareness.

2. What steps can you take to improve your self-awareness?

3. How aware are you of your moods, emotions, and drives?

4. How effective are you in recognizing your impact on others?

5. How self-disciplined are you? What causes you to lose control?

6. To what extent do you accept yourself? What is the source of your self-acceptance?

7. How self-confident are you? What is the basis for your self-confidence?

8. What might happen that could cause you to lose your self-confidence?

Allow fifteen to twenty minutes each for the responses to these questions.

TOPIC 6: YOUR VALUES

1. What are your cardinal values—those upon which you have built your life; those that guide your work and personal life; those that you follow in your professional, leadership, parental, and friendship roles?

2. What is the source of your values? How have they changed over time?

3. Reflecting on your life story, describe a situation in which you deviated from your values in order to achieve a goal. What caused this? What did you learn from the experience?

4. Recall a time when your values conflicted. How did you respond?

5. In what ways, if any, are you deviating at present from your values?

TOPIC 7: YOUR PASSIONS AND MOTIVATIONS

1. What are the main passions in your life?

2. What are the extrinsic, or external, factors that motivate you?

3. What are the intrinsic, or internal, factors that motivate you?

4. How well do you balance your intrinsic and extrinsic motivations?

5. What are the causes, issues, or challenges that excite and drive you?

6. What kind of work would you do if money were not an object?

7. What might you pursue in a future career?

TOPIC 8: YOUR TALENTS AND CAPABILITIES

1. What are your main skills and capabilities? (Think of capabilities as complex tasks you can perform with proficiency.)

2. What are your greatest strengths?

3. What are the areas that you have not yet fully developed or explored?

TOPIC 9: YOUR RELATIONSHIPS AND SUPPORT TEAM

1. Who have been the principal mentors, guides, coaches, teachers, teams, and groups in your life to date?

2. How have these relationships changed over time?

3. Who is on your support team? What additional people would you like to have on your support team?

4. Who are you confident would be there to support you when you are facing serious challenges?

5. Who are you most able to be open and intimate with? To what extent?

TOPIC 10: LIVING AN INTEGRATED LIFE

In the lives of busy and successful people, there are often unlimited pressures and demands. Your life never seems to be in perfect balance. It is extremely difficult to meet the needs of your family, your work, and your community while still reserving time for yourself.

You are in this group to grow and develop yourself. Sometimes the behaviors we use to achieve professional success run counter to success at home, with our health, or in our personal and spiritual lives.

Integrating our lives involves making hard choices. We use the term *integrating* as opposed to *balancing* because balance is an impossible goal if our primary vocation necessarily commands the bulk of our time. Living an integrated life means that you lead your life with integrity. This requires that, to the greatest extent possible, you are the same person at work, at home, by yourself, and in your community. The following questions may take as many as three sessions to discuss in depth.

Trade-Offs

1. What do you consider to be the most important elements in the following?:

   Professional life

   Personal life

   Family life

   Community life

   Friendships

2. What are the most important trade-offs you are currently making among these five categories?

   In this exercise, look at the time you allocate to each of

the five categories and how you would ideally like to be spending it.

Attention Given and Desired

CATEGORY	ATTENTION GIVEN (%)	ATTENTION DESIRED (%)
Professional life	_____	_____
Personal life	_____	_____
Family life	_____	_____
Community	_____	_____
Friends	_____	_____

1. What changes do you need to make to achieve the "attention desired" percentages?
2. What is keeping you from making these changes?

Body, Mind, and Spirit

A wise person once observed, "Unless you take care of yourself—your mind, body, and spirit—you will not be able to adequately take care of the rest of your responsibilities." What habits and practices do you employ to take care of and develop your

- Body
- Mind
- Spirit

TOPIC 11: YOUR LIFE'S PURPOSE

1. What is the purpose of your life at this time?

2. How does it correspond to your capabilities and your passions?

3. Are your life and your work aligned with your purpose?

4. What changes do you need to make to be aligned with your purpose?

TOPIC 12: EMPOWERING OTHERS

Growing up in your family, were you empowered by one or both of your parents? Can you recall the feeling of being trusted and treated as if you were lovable and capable?

When you are working on a team, committee, or project with someone else as leader, you hope to have the same experience. So do your associates when you are the leader. Empowered people achieve greater results and are more satisfied than others.

To help you in all the roles in which you interact with others, this session will encourage you to review your experiences, the lessons you learned from them, and your plans to improve your skills in applying empowerment principles.

1. What are your favorite memories about being empowered by others?

2. Describe a time when you were successful in empowering others.

3. What have you found to be the key elements in empowering others?

4. When have you been effective in challenging people to achieve more than they thought possible?

5. When have you been effective in sharing credit with your colleagues?

FEEDBACK SESSION

After completing this start-up curriculum, it is important to plan an entire session in which each group member can give and receive feedback from other group members. See Resource 6 for ground rules for feedback sessions.

FUTURE DISCUSSIONS

Participants should have an open discussion about the kinds of topics they would like to discuss in future programs. Resource 2 provides a list of ideas and topics that have worked well for other groups.

Additional Program Ideas

WHEN IT IS YOUR TURN TO FACILITATE YOUR GROUP, you have both the challenge and the opportunity to choose a topic for the group to discuss. Life presents an enormous portfolio of possibilities. Ensure that the topics you choose are in keeping with the practice of having members recount their experiences and behaviors rather than their opinions. Keep conversations in touch with the heart and the soul, not just the intellect.

The following topics have been successfully used by True North Groups and other groups.

PERSONAL EXPERIENCES

1. Money in your life: What role does money play in your life? How does your family handle discussions about money?

2. Seeing possibilities: When in your life have you "lit a candle rather than cursed the darkness"?

3. Early experiences: What preteen experiences were most important in shaping you?

4. Discrimination: When have you been discriminated against? How did that make you feel? Think of a time when you have discriminated against others. What were you feeling?

5. Mystical experiences: Have you ever had a mystical experience? What was it like?

PERSONAL BELIEFS

1. Living a full life: What does it mean to you to live a full life?

2. Life's essential questions: What are the most important questions facing you at this point?

3. Prejudices: What prejudices did you inherit from your family? How active are these in your life today? What new ones have you developed since you left your childhood home?

4. Meaning: In which sources in your life do you find meaning?

5. Risk taking: What risks do you wish you had taken in your life? In which areas of your life do you tend to take risks and where do you avoid them?

6. Fulfillment: What gives you fulfillment? How can you find more of this?

7. Passion: What issues are you passionate about today? Which ones are you no longer passionate about?

8. Life's mysteries: What are the mysteries for you in this life?

9. Heroes: Who are your heroes and why?

10. Personal creed: What is your personal creed—those truths and beliefs that guide who you are and what you try to be? How has this changed over the years, if at all? How does your personal creed give guidance and direction to your life?

11. Death: What are your feelings about your death? Are you prepared for it?

12. Making assumptions: What are your deepest assumptions about your family? Your colleagues? Your boss? Your competitors? People in general? Foreigners?

PERSONAL LEARNING

1. Courage: What role does courage play in your life now? Who taught you about courage? When have you been courageous? When do you wish you had been more courageous?

2. Staying grounded: What practices do you have in your life that help you stay grounded?

3. Pleasure and satisfaction: What are you most pleased about in your life so far?

4. Surprises: What have been the major surprises in your life? About yourself? About others? About the world? About life?

5. Anger: How often do you get angry? How does your anger manifest itself? What triggers your anger? How important is anger in your life today? Is it stronger than in years past? Who or what are the targets for your anger? To what degree is anger a choice in your life?

6. Priorities: What are the top priorities in your life at this time? Before you answer, consult your calendar, your checkbook, and your credit card purchases for the past six months. What are the patterns that show up? How do you feel about these? What changes would you wish to make?

7. Satisfaction: What is the greatest source of satisfaction in your life? Why? What are the areas where you are dissatisfied with your life?

ASPIRATIONS

1. Living a full life: In which aspects do you feel your life is most fully lived? In which is it not?

2. Following your True North: What are you like when you operate from your True North? When are you most at peace with yourself?

3. Desires: What do you hunger for or strongly desire at this point in your life?

4. Accomplishments: What do you hope to achieve in your remaining years?

5. Changing your life: In your remaining years, in what ways would you like to be different? What do you plan to do to accomplish these changes?

6. Inner desires: What inner desires do you have that are yet to be fulfilled?

7. Harmony: What do you have to do to achieve the desired sense of harmony in your life?

The Group's Initial Meeting

1. Welcome the attendees. Have everyone introduce themselves and share why they want to join this group.

2. Review the details of the group:

    How the group came together

    The group's purpose

    Initial goals for the group

    Proposed membership size and additional recruiting required

    Membership criteria and procedures to add new people

    Meeting length, frequency, location, and days and times

    Typical meeting format

    Handling of any expenses

3. Review the proposed member contract (see Resource 4). Since this establishes explicit norms for the group, it should be studied carefully. If everyone is in agreement, then each person should sign the document, indicating commitment to it. If not, then it can be finalized at the next meeting.

4. Decide on the leadership structure to be used, whether the group is to be peer facilitated, professionally facilitated, or permanently facilitated by a group member (see Chapter 3 and Resource 7).

5. Confirm the next meeting and hand out the initial discussion topic for the next meeting on early life experiences. Some groups schedule enough time to begin this
topic at the first meeting.

Member Contract

Confidentiality

I commit to maintaining strict confidentiality about what is said in all group sessions and in any discussions with group members away from the group sessions. This includes sharing any information or observations with nonmembers, whether colleagues, partners, spouses, or friends.

Openness

I commit to being open in sharing highly personal matters with members of the group, with the understanding that everything will be held in strictest confidence. If others are not sharing openly with the group, it is my responsibility to raise this with them for discussion within the group. I agree not to push individuals beyond their comfort zone on personally sensitive matters.

Trust

I will join this group with the assumption that its members are worthy of trust. I understand that trust is built through honest, open communications and caring for other members of the group.

Listening

I commit to practicing active listening and to avoid interrupting the member speaking.

Judging Others

I commit to withholding judgment of group members and will avoid giving them unsolicited advice. I will not try to impose my values and beliefs on other members.

Feedback

As a group member, I will offer and receive constructive feedback from others in the group on ideas, behavior, leadership traits, and communication styles.

Attendance

I will make every effort to attend all meetings and retreats scheduled for the group, to be on time, and to not leave early unless there are extenuating circumstances.

Member's signature: _____ Date:_____

(*Note:* This contract should be reviewed and updated annually.)

Meeting Formats

TYPICAL MEETING AGENDA

1. At the appointed hour, the facilitator invites the group to begin the meeting. If some members are late, it is an important norm to begin the session on time.

2. If there is a norm to have an opening ritual, like a prayer, poem, or reading, it should be used to open the meeting.

3. The facilitator asks the group if anyone has an important issue or experience they want to share at the outset. If so, this should take precedence and should be discussed to a reasonable point of conclusion. However, this part of the meeting should not be allowed to drift into discussing current events or social issues.

4. The facilitator begins the discussion by framing the topic for the meeting and asking the opening question. The facilitator continues the session along this line.

5. If the group uses a closing ritual, the facilitator will bring the discussion to an end prior to the closing time and move to the closing ritual.

6. Before the group separates, the facilitator should remind the group of the next meeting date, time, and location, especially if there are any changes pending. This is also the time for members to announce if they will be missing the next meeting.

OPENING RITUALS

1. Your group may or may not choose to open its meetings with an opening ritual. This tradition can help set the proper framework and mood for the group's meeting and also serves as a more formal reminder that the meeting has begun.

2. If your group does not choose to have an opening ritual, you may move directly into the meeting program.

3. In its early meetings, your group may want to experiment with a number of different openings before selecting one. Some groups leave that choice to the facilitator of a particular meeting. Others use several rituals that are rotated over time. Some suggested opening rituals include:

    A period of silence or meditation for a period of one to three minutes

    A prayer, either the same one every week or one offered by the facilitator

    A poem or a short story chosen to illustrate the topic of the day

    Each member gives a one-word description of where they are in their lives that day

CLOSING RITUALS

1. Gather in a standing circle to remember friends or relatives who are going through difficulties and to offer needed support for individuals in the group.

2. Members have a standing prayer or saying they use to close the meeting.

3. The facilitator offers a poem or reading to conclude the meeting.

4. Members offer a word or a thought to capture what they are taking away from that particular meeting.

5. If the group meets monthly or less, there can be a two- to three-minute check-in by each member. This is recommended for the close of the meeting because otherwise this can expand to take over half of the meeting.

Ground Rules for Group Discussions

FOR YOUR TRUE NORTH GROUP TO ENGAGE IN MEAN-
ingful, personal, and intimate discussions, it is especially
important to establish ground rules for group discussions.
The goal for your group is to engage in honest conversations.

When you tell your group about a situation or event
in your life, you deserve to be listened to receptively and
respectfully. You want others to try to understand what is
happening and to help you clarify the situation. You are not
looking for judgments, arguments, advice, or fixes at that
moment. You expect others to listen with their hearts and
not try to change you or the situation.

Nor do you want to be cross-examined or ganged up upon.
Sometimes you prefer to have some quiet time between each
person who speaks, so you can digest what you have just
heard. You don't want to be chastised. You are not looking
for a debate or for someone to point out how you might have
avoided a painful situation. Sometimes you just want your
friends to surround you with their care.

Isn't this exactly what other people want and need from
you when they share something deeply personal to them?

This is a good example to guide you in your actions and
responses in your True North Group. How you listen within
your group is as important as what you say. Ask honest,
open-ended questions to learn more and to clarify the matter, rather than trying to lead the person toward your way
of thinking. Don't try to fix, save, or blame the speaker. You

and your colleagues are there to help another person become clearer about their situation with your active and supportive listening, not to solve all their problems.

A useful assumption to make is that people can eventually reach a resolution to their situation with the assistance of gentle, supportive listening and open-ended and clarifying questions.

Here are some suggestions for how a meaningful group discussion works:

1. Everyone is talking on-point.
2. They are building on the comments of other group members.
3. All are sharing openly and personally.
4. People are actively listening to others.
5. Members share their feelings honestly.
6. People disagree respectfully.
7. Facilitators bring the discussion back to the topic if it begins to wander.
8. No one is dominating the discussion.
9. The facilitator ensures adherence to the group norms.

If the discussions in your True North Group follow these guidelines, you will enjoy the benefits of having honest conversations.

Guide for Facilitating Groups

SOUND FACILITATION OF YOUR TRUE NORTH GROUP IS
an essential element of its effectiveness and its ability to
engage in honest conversations that are useful for all its
members.

First, your group should decide on the leadership model
you intend to use. The three models described in the chapter on forming were peer facilitators, professional facilitators,
and group member as permanent facilitator. This resource
provides a complete guide to facilitating groups as a peer and
to finding a professional facilitator.

MEMBER-LED GROUPS WITH PEER FACILITATORS

One of the most important skills every group member should
have in a peer-led group is the ability to facilitate effectively.
Whatever your life role, at some point you will be called
upon to facilitate a group. Many people have had experience
in facilitating and leading task-oriented groups, but facilitating a True North Group is considerably different from leading a task team.

In your True North Group, the emphasis is on the personal, not on accomplishing a task or having intellectual discussions. In these groups you will be addressing personal
topics, and the task is to know yourself better, to enable other
group members to understand themselves, and to build trust
and bonding within the group.

Facilitating a group of this type requires a level of skill to draw out personal experiences and ensure that insights and reflections are drawn from all participants. The facilitator must establish an atmosphere of trust and openness that enables group members to share openly.

It is important to emphasize that True North Groups are not therapy groups or 1960s T-groups. Facilitators are not asked to act as a psychologist or therapist. It is imperative that a safe atmosphere exists at all times. That said, it is equally important that all group members feel they are getting their fair share of airtime, without one or more members dominating the group. Nor is it acceptable if individuals refrain from full participation in the group or withdraw during the sharing process.

YOUR ROLE AS FACILITATOR

When you lead a True North Group session, you are helping to build the community of which you are now a member. Important life change happens within the bounds of intentional growth relationships such as these. Your role as facilitator may be different from any you have had before. Your goal is to encourage all group members to open up and share personal stories, beliefs, and principles. To facilitate a fruitful discussion, you should encourage people to speak from their hearts, not their heads.

To *facilitate* means "to make easier." As a facilitator, your job is to make the conversation among your colleagues freer and more satisfying. Ensure the atmosphere is relaxed, safe, noncompetitive, and conducive to sharing. Usually, this means beginning the discussion by asking the opening question and then withholding your input until others have spoken. You guide the discussion to ensure all have the opportunity to speak and that no one dominates.

In this role you are neither the teacher nor the expert or scorekeeper. Your role is to listen carefully to what is said, to help guide the discussion so that everyone is heard, to ensure that no one dominates, and to enable group members to share differing opinions in a respectful manner.

Tight control is the enemy of open sharing. Pushing hard to accomplish fixed goals you have for the session can keep you from creating an open dialogue. Still, you have things to accomplish and a timetable to maintain. Your job requires that your group achieve a balance between task accomplishment and a collegial, open climate that builds trust. This won't be as formless or free-flowing as a social gathering of your group nor as structured as a task team with measurable outcomes.

CHOOSING DISCUSSION TOPICS

During your group's first year, it is important to use the start-up curriculum. Begin by carefully going over the topics and instructions presented in Resource 1. Then refer to the corresponding chapter in *True North* to get some deeper insights about the topic. You may want to assign this chapter as reading for your members. You will also find some proven exercises aligned with this topic in *Finding Your True North: A Personal Guide*.

After the first year, you can get ideas for additional programs by studying the list presented in Resource 2 and choosing a topic. Or you may come up with a topic of your own. Then develop a key question that you will use to initiate the discussion, followed by other questions you want the group to address. These should be open-ended questions that cannot be answered with yes or no. We suggest that questions start with the words *who, what, why, where, when,* or *how.*

It is helpful to share in advance with members the questions to be addressed. If you plan to use a reading, it is a good idea to e-mail it to group members so you do not have to use discussion time for everyone to read it. You should arrive early to ensure the room is organized the way you want it in order to promote sharing.

Always start with a welcome that makes everyone feel comfortable about being in the group. Follow this with any introductory comments and announcements.

As facilitator, you may want to offer the opportunity at the outset for group members to check in by taking a minute or two to share with the other members anything significant in their lives since the last meeting, or members might speak about what they are feeling at that moment. Such time can build trust, especially in early meetings. Due to time constraints, however, this part of the discussion should not be allowed to drag on unless the issues raised are extremely serious. If the group likes to chat too much, it will detract from the group discussion. Alternatively, you can reserve this part of the discussion for the end.

As facilitator, it is your responsibility to keep the group on task in a pleasant, efficient manner, making sure everyone has the opportunity to participate and no one dominates the discussion. Your goal is to have a discussion with full participation that results in honest conversation.

A worthwhile and satisfying discussion about highly personal topics hinges on the chemistry of the group and the mood of the meeting. Usually, you will not be in a crisis mode, so it should be fairly easy to keep the mood relaxed, open, friendly, and comfortable for all group members. Appropriate humor from time to time can help set the tone and can break the ice if the discussion is getting too tense or emotional.

To begin the substance of the discussion, pose the open-ended question that each member should answer and let whoever is prepared to speak go first. Alternatively, you can volunteer to go first, serving as a role model in answering the question in an open manner. It is recommended that you give each person an allotted amount of time to respond to the opening question, and let everyone share their responses before you open up the discussion to a broader dialogue. Otherwise, you may run out of time for everyone to respond.

In this kind of round-robin, listening skills are very important. It is sometimes hard to keep an open mind during the discussions, as members may want to evaluate and respond to the speaker. Your job is to listen actively to each person and, if necessary, lead the discussion in the appropriate direction. You should encourage response or support for each speaker before moving on. Make the discussion lively by keeping the group moving and engaged in the topic.

THINGS TO WATCH FOR DURING THE MEETING

1. Keeping your group on track. In select instances, you may have to act like a timekeeper to keep the discussion flowing. There will be times when you have to gently interrupt a dominator by asking a quiet member of your group to respond. In other cases, you may have to guide the discussion back to the central point. There will be times when you have to move to another topic or person in spite of some who want to continue with the current discussion. There will be cases when the group will seem to lose interest in a topic and you must shift prematurely to another subject to keep the momentum of the discussion lively and fresh.

2. Balancing group participation. You will have to pay close attention to what is being said and not said. What are the nonverbal signals being sent in addition to those vocally shared? This is a skill that takes time to develop and sharpen. Is the quality of the discussion superficial or deep? How much are you talking? How involved are the other members? Be sure that everyone gets adequate airtime and doesn't just pull back into themselves.

3. Dealing with a dominant group member. You may be aware of a group member who begins to monopolize the discussion. You may have to cut him or her off tactfully but firmly and shift to someone who is not as verbal. If you see this behavior continue, a private comment to the person after the meeting is in order.

4. Your active leadership. Pay attention to your own energy level. It is relatively easy to get off to a strong beginning as you have adrenaline working in your favor. If you aren't a little nervous and keyed up at the start, then perhaps you are taking your responsibilities too casually. On the other hand, keeping sharp during the entire meeting and listening in a new, unfamiliar way can be tiring. Try to pace yourself to maintain a solid, active presence.

5. Staying on time. Few highly effective meetings work on a tight timetable, which tends to suppress deeper conversations. Use your judgment about how loose or tight the whole process needs to be. There may be a time when you sense the group needs to take a short pause. Having everyone stand and stretch for a minute can help jump-start a discussion that needs refreshing. Your group will develop its own norms for breaks and refreshments. Use these judiciously to instill renewed energy into the session. At the end, you can feel satisfaction in having led a meaningful and rich discussion.

USING A PROFESSIONAL FACILITATOR

The key to making the professional facilitator model work effectively is to find one who is both skilled and experienced in leading groups like True North Groups. This role is so vital that it is important to find a professional rather than turning to a friend who may have had some facilitating experience. The following are some suggestions for finding the right facilitator.

Facilitators, especially professional ones, are as important to your group as members. Thus, it is extremely important to ensure that they fit with the members of your group or those you are trying to attract. Start-up facilitators will set an early tone for the group that must be positive.

In looking for a professional facilitator, you may begin by contacting the chapter of a professional coaching association in your area. Call the staff person who runs the association to determine whether they know of some coaches who also have group facilitation experience. If so, obtain a few of those names that fit your criteria for gender and experience and interview candidates.

Another source is guidance and counseling departments in nearby colleges or universities. Likewise, many psychologists and psychiatrists are trained to facilitate groups. These latter resources may be more expensive.

Be sure to have a written agreement with your facilitator regarding the length of the engagement, the process for review and renewal of the engagement, and how the remuneration will be handled. Facilitator attendance and timeliness are important, especially in a short-term arrangement, so manage them closely.

HAVING A GROUP MEMBER AS PERMANENT FACILITATOR

If your group decides to select one of your members to be permanent facilitator, it is essential to get the ground rules established at the outset. Will the facilitator be paid or do the work pro bono? You should set a time limit on that person's leadership—say, one year—and then have an honest assessment at the end of the period.

Another key question is whether the member-facilitator will be an active member of the group, participating equally in all group discussions, or will take a more passive role, as a professional facilitator would do. Finally, you need to establish that all the group members are comfortable with this member's lead role and do not feel diminished by it.

SUMMARY

In our research, we have seen that all three facilitation models can work well. The choice should be based upon the makeup of the group and the preference of the members. If, after a reasonable period of time, the facilitation model you have chosen does not seem to be working, it is a good idea to shift to one of the other models.

Having a member-led group with peer facilitators has several advantages that make it our preference. You will find member engagement and commitment increase with involvement, whereas dependence on other facilitators can cause some members to become more like spectators. Although this model can experience some shaky early performance, over time it is the one that helps share the load of keeping the group sharp and builds equality among members.

Member Satisfaction Survey

IT IS WISE TO TAKE THE TEMPERATURE OF YOUR MEMBERS each year in order to determine their level of satisfaction. This may be done orally or in writing. The written survey may bring out comments that people hesitate to say in front of the whole group.

This survey can be as elaborate or as simple as the need requires. In groups without major storming issues, the simplified survey suggested below can assist in taking the pulse of the members. In addition, it can help identify suggestions to be considered for improved group functioning.

Usually once a year, either around the anniversary of the group's formation or at a retreat held near this date, have one of your members gather the completed surveys to study the results. We suggest all the answers to each question be gathered without identification and put on a single page. Then, the group should discuss collectively the responses to each question to see if there are things your group should reemphasize, continue, or drop. Most members will acknowledge their responses. If there are negative comments about one or more specific members, you may want to hold those back until a feedback session and ensure they are brought forth then.

It is a good idea to compare the current results with those of prior years to see what trends may appear. You will want to pay special attention to the satisfaction question in comparison to prior years. Don't stop the discussion until all of the major issues have been discussed and resolved the best they can be at that time. Some may well be carried over for further study and thought.

The following is a suggested format for a member satisfaction survey.

TRUE NORTH GROUP MEMBER SURVEY

1. What does our group mean to you?

2. What are its main strengths? What should we take forward?

3. What should we leave behind?

4. What are things about the group that bother you?

5. What should we add/begin?

6. Who should we consider as potential members?

7. Anything else?

8. Circle the words that represent your satisfaction with the group:

   Very Satisfied   Neither Satisfied   Very Dissatisfied
                       nor Dissatisfied

9. Please explain your rating:

_____

_____

_____

_____

_____

_____

_____

_____

Your Name: _____ Date: _____

Group Retreats

TAKING AN ANNUAL RETREAT IS AN INTEGRAL PART OF the process of many True North Groups. Retreats provide time together to build group chemistry and discuss important topics in greater depth. Most often, retreats take place over a weekend, when work commitments are less likely to intervene.

Retreats can be held anywhere that is conducive to relaxed conversations and provides opportunities for group activities. Suggested sites include a member's cabin or second home, a retreat center, a resort, or a bed-and-breakfast. It is preferable that the group have the entire place to itself, although that is not always possible for small groups.

One of the members should take the initiative to develop the program for the group's discussion. Several of the members may lead different portions of the agenda. If the retreat lasts two or three days, it can be effective to utilize a multipart program, with each part building on the prior topic. In this way, the group can go much deeper into a topic than it can in its regular meetings.

Retreats are also an excellent time to review the group's process and individual members' satisfaction with the group. If the group has completed a written member satisfaction survey, the retreat is the perfect time to discuss it. Alternatively, the survey can be taken during the retreat itself. This is an excellent time to discuss any changes members would like to see in the group's process. The group can also brainstorm ideas and generate a list of future programs.

Another opportunity for retreats is to use the time for individual feedback sessions, as the more relaxed environment increases the likelihood that members will be open to the feedback and have opportunities to ask questions about it.

The feedback we received from members we interviewed during our research process suggests that retreats are fun, encourage deeper conversation, and lead to bonding among group members. They also offer the chance to get to know your colleagues in different settings and to build a stronger community. One interviewee shared her favorite retreat experience, noting, "Each of us brought our favorite poem to share with the group." She continued,

> We were in a beautiful garden on a warm spring day. As we read them aloud, the poems took on a different sense of meaning. Unpacking these poems together and reflecting on them was a deeply spiritual experience. The mixed-gender responses added a different energy and flavor to them. We each shared why our particular poem was so important to us. It was an experience I will treasure forever.

As Eric Utne notes, "The value of a retreat is that you get to know each other much better."

> You have time to hang out, take walks, and have one-on-ones with others that you cannot have in regular meetings. Preparing food and doing dishes helps you find ways to work together and connect in new ways.

Suggested True North Group exercises for retreats focus on self-revelation about your experiences, your values, your relationships, and how all these have shaped who you have become. This ultimately leads to any changes you want to make to become more of the person you seek to be. Other questions might include:

1. What are the changes you want to make regarding your mind? Your body? Your spirit?

2. Taking stock of your life at this point, what's next?

3. How will you know when you have what you need and want?

4. What more do you have to prove? To whom?

5. What are the major gifts you will need to use in the next chapter of your life?

6. What's being born in you now? What's dying in you now?

7. What was the most important advice given to you and by whom?

8. What is the most important gift you have received? What is the most important gift you have given?

9. Reflecting on when you were seven years old, what would that youngster think about who you have become?

Adding New Members
to Existing Groups

AT SOME POINT, YOUR TRUE NORTH GROUP WILL HAVE to replace some of its members, as people move out of town or resign from the group, or you may want to expand your group's size. In our experience, it is much more difficult to add new members to an existing group than it is to form the group in the first place.

Once a group bonds, which usually occurs during the first eighteen months of its existence, it often becomes difficult for the group to accept new members. This may emanate from the close bond forged by the members, who are reluctant to risk disturbing the group's chemistry. Others may not want to take the time to bring new members up to speed. For these reasons it is essential to have all existing members in agreement about additions before initiating the process of selecting new members.

On an annual basis, the group should discuss whether there is a need and interest in expanding the membership. This can be done at a retreat or a regular meeting. If so, the original criteria established for membership should be reviewed and discussed to see if they are still relevant. Then the members can decide how to proceed.

Often there will be names of prospects that quickly surface, some of whom may have expressed an interest in joining the group. If enough members are familiar with the individuals, then a ranking vote can be held to determine the order in which the prospects will be considered. The group can also discuss whether there should be a trial period offered to the prospect to confirm the interest of both sides.

Then a group of two or three members should visit with the candidate to confirm the fit for both the group and the individual. If all goes well, an invitation can be extended at that time.

An alternative approach is for two existing members to take the lead in seeking new members. They will act as a search team, setting the criteria and demographics for candidates and developing the process to gather names from existing members and screen candidates. After speaking with the candidates, the two members report back to the members and decisions are taken. When the new members join the group, these two members can act as mentors to them.

Some of the people you invite to join your group may already be friends of group members. There will be others suggested, however, who no one knows well, if at all. In this case, you may wish to use the following as a template to get more biographical information about them and about why they are interested in joining your group.

TRUE NORTH GROUP CANDIDATE BIOGRAPHY

Name_____

Home address _____

Cell phone_____

Work phone _____

E-mail address _____

Current employer/role/dates
(if retired, most recent employer/role)

Postsecondary education

Continuing education activities

Your age cohort (circle):   20 to 35   36 to 55   56+

Community/organizational leadership roles/dates

How did you learn about True North Groups?

What is your interest in such a group?

Small group experience. Please list the primary purpose of each group, number of years of involvement, the value of group to you, and your reason for leaving, if appropriate.

What is your life's purpose at this point?

Anything else we should know about you?

Signature: _____ Date: _____

Please mail/fax/e-mail to: _____

Giving and Receiving Feedback

PREPARATION

Feedback sessions are intended to help rather than to criticize individual members of your group. One of the hardest things to do is to see yourself as others see you. It can be difficult to find people who will give you honest, thoughtful feedback, uncolored by their own desires or biases.

Another important benefit of feedback sessions is the opportunity to build a stronger, more cohesive group. Feedback sessions are not intended in any way to punish or harm your colleagues; if that happens, the group has created a serious breach.

What are the important messages you want your colleagues to hear? Why are these important? Will they help them become stronger people and better leaders?

As the provider of feedback, you need to be clear about your purpose. Are you genuinely trying to help the recipient, or are there feelings within you that would like to punish the other person? Are your comments delivered in such a way that they are likely to be heard and received, or will they be ignored or rejected? How can you express yourself so that your messages will be taken in by the other person?

SETTING THE STAGE

It is essential to have the entire group together when you share feedback. It is even better to plan feedback for a retreat, when you have ample time to give each member adequate attention. Set aside time for the members to prepare their notes privately before the session.

This exercise should be scheduled early in the day, when everyone is fresh. Avoid serving alcohol or conducting this exercise just before you end the meeting. If there are particularly tough messages that may be given, be sure to allot time together to process as a group the feedback people have received.

When offering feedback, it is useful to have members first give their assessment of themselves, followed by the responses of others, who will concur or provide their own views.

POSSIBLE GROUP FEEDBACK TOPICS

1. Individual feedback to all members about their contributions
2. Effectiveness and openness of group discussions
3. Inputs about specific programs and potential topics
4. Interactions within the group
5. Ways to improve group chemistry and bonding
6. Perceived violations of group norms
7. Concerns about individual behaviors, attitudes, or participation
8. Checking out individual desires for group direction

Research Process

IN 2007, WE INITIATED THE RESEARCH STUDY ON SMALL groups that led to the publication of *True North Groups.* Researcher Jane Cavanaugh, who has been a member of several small groups, joined the team that year to assist in the research process and to conduct interviews of group members.

RESEARCH FOR TRUE NORTH GROUPS

During the past three years, members of the research team have conducted an extensive literature search and Web-based analysis of existing small groups of the types listed in Chapter 1. They have investigated many small groups similar to True North Groups across the United States and have met in person with organizers of these groups.

A formal process for interviewing members of these groups was initiated in 2007. Fifty-two participants were formally interviewed, with notes taken and transcripts made of each interview. The interviews lasted for seventy-five minutes on average. Quotations from the interviewees provide significant content and insights throughout the book. The list of interviewees and their career positions is provided here.

The findings from this research process form the basis for this book. The principle finding from the formal interviews and the investigation of other small groups was that the participants in these groups were uniformly positive about their experiences. Although their reasons for these favorable reactions varied significantly from one participant to the next, that did not take away from the positive nature of the descriptions of their groups. This finding was applicable to a variety of the groups investigated. No attempt was made to quantify the degree of favorability of groups or to rank them based on their feedback. Nevertheless, the research team concluded that the degree of positivity was both significant and meaningful in their lives.

Based on our research and interviewees, the authors concluded that nonaligned small groups have unique benefits that can be replicated and experienced across a wide range of participants, provided the appropriate structure is put in place at the outset.

INTERVIEWEES FOR TRUE NORTH GROUPS

The following people were interviewed for *True North Groups:*

Cheryl Alexander, CEO, Cheryl Alexander & Associates Inc.

Monica Alvarez, director of Forum, Young Presidents' Organization

Carole Baker, interior designer, yoga teacher

Frank Bennett, chaplain, Abbott Northwestern Hospital

Mary Birchard, executive director, Alzheimer's Association, MN-Dakotas

Bruce Carlson, real estate development

Norman Carpenter, attorney-at-law (retired)

Jane Cavanaugh, founder, retreat director, The Vineyard

Joe Cavanaugh, founder, CEO, Youth Frontiers Inc.

Kim Culp, CEO and president, The Excelsior Group

John Cuningham, founder, chair, The Cuningham Group

Dwight Cummins, attorney-at-law

Ted Cushmore, senior vice president, General Mills Inc. (retired)

John Curtiss, president and CEO, The Retreat

Chuck Denny, CEO, ADC Telecommunications (retired)

David Duclos, senior securities analyst, Dain Bosworth (retired)

Dave Dustrud, JD, MDiv

Karla Ekdahl, community activist, volunteer

Ted Forbes, vice president, General Mills Inc. (retired)

Dee Gaeddert, vice president, Korn/Ferry International

Dr. Penny George, president, George Family Foundation

Peter Gillette, president, Northwestern National Bank (retired)

David Hansen, CEO, Spancrete (retired)

Dr. Paul Harris, pastor, Eastern Lutheran Church

Rick Heltne, senior consultant, People Management and SIMA
    International

Olivia Hoblitzelle, author

Loren Hoyman, psychologist

Fred Kiel, partner, KRW Consulting Psychologists

Laura Kinkead, consultant

Ron Kirscht, president, Donnelly Custom Manufacturing Company

Ross Levin, senior partner, Accredited Investors

Joyce McFarland, community volunteer

Jonathan Morgan, attorney-at-law (retired)

Craig Neal, cofounder, Heartland Institute

Diane Nettifee, president, Magis Ventures

Carol Olson Johnson, president, COJ Resources

Jim Pfau, entrepreneur

Karen Radtke, assistant vice president, Equity Residential

Dick Rice, counselor, The Retreat

Delia Seeberg, legal assistant, Hughes Socol Piers Resnick &
    Dym Ltd.

Mike Seaman, teacher, Highland Elementary School

Tom Schaefer, retired business executive, community volunteer

Dave Scherf, president, Scherf Construction

Jack Sell, group chair, Vintage International

Gary Smaby, managing partner, Square One Ventures

Paul Strickland, vice president, Target Corp. (retired)

Maureen Swan, president, MedTrend Inc.

Buddy Tester, formerly director of Forum, Young Presidents' Organization

Lynn Truesdell, attorney-at-law (retired)

Eric Utne, founder, *Utne Reader*

Ron Vantine, retired business lawyer

Dr. Kathryn Williams, partner, KRW Consulting Psychologists

RESEARCH ON HARVARD'S LEADERSHIP DEVELOPMENT GROUPS

The True North Group model has been used extensively in the Authentic Leadership Development course designed by Professor Bill George as an elective for MBAs at Harvard Business School. These groups are called Leadership Development Groups (LDGs), but their structure and content are virtually identical to the True North Groups described here. Since the initiation of the Authentic Leadership Development course in 2005, more than 1,100 MBAs have been members of LDGs. The LDGs have consistently been rated the most important part of the course and are cited as the reason for the extremely large number of applicants.

Under Bill George's supervision, a detailed study of twenty-nine LDG participants was conducted in the spring of 2008 by a three-person team of graduate students—Amanda Levary, Katie Shaw, and Ira Nobel. Each of the interviews was transcribed. Specific comments from interviewees gave added insights into why they valued the LDG process so highly. The study also offered insights and recommendations for making LDGs even more effective and was helpful in the formulation of the processes needed for True North Groups.

Since 2009, LDGs have been used in the Global Leadership and Public Policy in the Twenty-First Century program at the Harvard Kennedy School, for Young Global Leaders of the World Economic Forum, who are in their thirties. Over two hundred people have participated in LDGs through this program. More recently, LDGs were used in the executive education version of the Authentic Leadership Development course, where participants range from thirty to sixty years of age. Measured by participant evaluations, the degree of positivity is even higher among midcareer participants.

A TYPOLOGY OF GROUPS BASED ON OPENNESS AND INTIMACY

All of the groups examined, other than those that have characteristics similar to True North Groups, have some form of affinity that initially brings them together: shared beliefs, common interests and/or concerns, and similar backgrounds. What makes True North Groups unique is the lack of such affinity. Some True North Groups have initially come together due to an affinity, but they evolve well beyond it over time.

Given the wide range of groups examined, the authors decided to create a typology of these groups (shown in Chapter 1), based on the degree of openness and intimacy expected in each type of group. This criterion was chosen based on interview findings, which suggested that openness and intimacy were the key metrics in determining groups' importance to their members and the longevity of their groups. It does not suggest that True North Groups are superior to other types of groups; rather, it indicates that, on the whole, such groups tend to achieve a higher degree of openness and intimacy across the full range of life's issues.

The authors' working hypothesis, which requires further examination and study, is that openness and intimacy are essential elements that can be used to measure the effectiveness of the group experience. Effectiveness, in this case, is measured by the degree of personal growth and development resulting from participation in the group, the shared experience of the group, and the level of feedback shared among group members. Although these metrics were not measured in this research, the authors postulate that these factors lead to the unusually high level of bonding among groups, especially those that have withstood the test of time and have shared a variety of life experiences. These hypotheses will require further study before they can be confirmed definitively.

1. Mary Oliver, "The Summer Day," *New and Selected Poems* (Boston: Beacon Press, 1992), 94.

2. Robert D. Putnam, *Bowling Alone: The Collapse and Revival of American Community* (New York: Simon & Schuster, 2000), 402.

3. John T. Cacioppo and William Patrick, *Loneliness: Human Nature and the Need for Social Connection* (New York: W. W. Norton & Company, 2008), 248–69.

4. Bruce W. Tuckman, "Developmental Sequence in Small Groups," *Psychology Bulletin* 63 (1965): 384–99.

5. Malcolm Gladwell, "The Cellular Church," *The New Yorker*, September 2005.

6. Conversation between Willow Creek Community Church Senior Pastor Bill Hybels, Willow Creek Leadership Summit Executive Director Steve Spoelhof, and Bill George, South Barrington, Illinois, May 16, 2008.

7. Abraham H. Maslow, *Motivation and Personality* (New York: Harper, 1954).

8. Daniel Goleman, *Working with Emotional Intelligence* (New York: Bantam Dell, 1998).

9. E-mail from Daniel Goleman to Bill George, January 14, 2011.

10. David Gergen, "Introduction," in *True North: Discover Your Authentic Leadership* (San Francisco: Jossey-Bass, 2007).

11. Student field research study by Amanda Levary, Katie Shaw, and Ira Nobel, under the supervision of Professor Bill George, Harvard Business School, Boston, April 2008.

12. See http://www.quotationspage.com/quotes/Woody_Allen.

Block, Peter. *Community*. San Francisco: Berrett-Koehler, 2008.

Cacioppo, John T., and William Patrick. *Loneliness: Human Nature and the Need for Social Connection*. New York: W. W. Norton & Company, 2008.

Leider, Richard. *The Power of Purpose: Creating Meaning in Your Life and Work*. San Francisco: Berrett-Koehler, 1997.

Leider, Richard, and David Shapiro. *Repacking Your Bags*. San Francisco: Berrett-Koehler, 1999.

McBride, Neal F. *How to Have Great Small-Group Meetings*. Colorado Springs, CO: NavPress, 1997.

Miller, James E. *Effective Support Groups*. Fort Wayne, IN: Willowgreen Publishing, 1998.

Palmer, Parker J. *A Hidden Wholeness*. San Francisco: Jossey-Bass, 2004.

Putnam, Robert D. *Bowling Alone: The Collapse and Revival of American Community*. New York: Simon & Schuster, 2000.

Stanley, Andy, and Bill Willits. *Creating Community*. Sisters, OR: Multnomah Publishers, 2004.

ACKNOWLEDGMENTS

Doug Baker says:

Just as there are no self-made people, no book is a solo effort. In my case, the numerous relatives, coaches, teachers, colleagues, clients, and partners over the years who helped teach and guide me are legion. At the top of the entire cast are my wife, Carole, and our family. Of particular note are the people in my various groups and teams. My eternal gratitude goes out to one and all.

Bill George's deep and long friendship has been an important facet of my life. Working together on this project has been most rewarding. Bill is an excellent teacher who willingly and quickly shares his wisdom.

Jane Leyden Cavanaugh is a treasure whose deep and incisive interviews provided many of the quotes and stories in this book. In so many ways, she has made this journey a joy.

Key contributors are all those interviewed for this book who are listed in the research section. We are grateful for their time and the wisdom they shared.

Steve Piersanti and his marvelous associates at Berrett-Koehler have made this venture educational, interesting, and enjoyable. My hat is off to them all. Four of BK's authors were very helpful in providing reviews of a later draft, which were very valuable.

Richard Leider, who put us in touch with BK. His foreword is a wonderful addition to this book.

To George Johnson for encouraging me to keep on with this project when things looked dark.

My colleagues Carrie Johnson and Sharon Thorson, who

are helping with the development of the True North Groups Institute.

In addition to the members and facilitators in our groups, others whose ideas, suggestions, and effort have been most helpful include Elise Bohaty, Dennis Coyne, Karla Ekdahl, Barry Fernald, David Kamminga, Fred Kiel, Susan Kinder, Laura Kinkead, Craig Neal, Patricia Neal, Stacy O'Keeffe, Carol Pine, Dan Rudd, Jim Smith, Dan Sundin, Diane Weinhold, Arwen Wilder, and Wilson Yates.

> Many thanks,
> Doug

Bill George says:

I am grateful to my wife, Penny, for all her encouragement, insights, and editing of this book, without which it would not have been possible. I also express my deep gratitude to the members of my men's group—John Cuningham, Chuck Denny, Peter Gillette, Jonathan Morgan, Tom Schaefer, and Ron Vantine—and our couples group—Carole Baker, Polly and Bob McCrea, and Cindy and Tad Piper—from whom I have learned so much about being a constructive member of their groups and who have provided so much love and caring as we have journeyed together down life's path for more than thirty years.

My coauthor, Doug Baker, was a treasure to work with, as I have learned so much from him about group process and leadership over many years. Jane Leyden Cavanaugh did a superb job in conducting many of the interviews of group members and providing useful insights about her group experiences. Along with Doug, I want to express my appreciation to Richard Leider for his thoughtful foreword.

I am most grateful to my Harvard Business colleagues Dean Nitin Nohria, Rob Kaplan, Scott Snook, and Joshua Margolis for their insights and efforts in teaching Authentic Leadership Development with me and for making the six-person Leadership Development Groups so effective. Diana Mayer at New York University, Bill Gunn and Terry Blum at Georgia Tech, and Iris Bonnet at Harvard Kennedy School have demonstrated that this process is transportable and replicable.

We received great support and insights from Steve Piersanti and his team at Berrett-Koehler, along with the book's reviewers, which included my good friend Ben Beaird. My office manager, Diane Weinhold, provided incisive editing and constructive suggestions for the book, along with excellent support from Kathy Farren, Dan Sundin, Stacy O'Keeffe, and Caitlin Weixel.

I also want to express my appreciation to all the people who shared with us about their groups in the interview process, whose quotes make up such an important part of this book.

> My sincere thanks to all of you,
> Bill

BILL GEORGE

Bill is professor of management practice at Harvard Business School, where he has taught leadership since 2004. He is the author of four best-selling books: *True North, Authentic Leadership, Finding Your True North,* and *7 Lessons for Leading in Crisis.*

He is former chairman and chief executive officer of Medtronic. He joined Medtronic in 1989 as president and chief operating officer, was CEO from 1991 to 2001, and served as board chair from 1996 to 2002. Earlier in his career, he was executive vice president of Honeywell, president of Litton Microwave Cooking Products, and served in the U.S. Department of Defense as special assistant to the Secretary of the Navy.

He currently serves as a director of ExxonMobil and Goldman Sachs, and recently served on the boards of Novartis and Target Corporation. He is a trustee of the Carnegie Endowment for International Peace, the World Economic Forum USA, and Tyrone Guthrie Theater.

Bill was named one of Top 25 Business Leaders of the Past 25 Years in 2004 by PBS; Executive of the Year 2001 by the Academy of Management; and Director of the Year 2001–02 by the National Association of Corporate Directors. He has made frequent appearances on television and radio, and his articles have appeared in *BusinessWeek, The Economist, Fortune, Harvard Business Review, The New York Times, The Wall Street Journal,* and other publications.

He received his BS in industrial engineering with high honors from Georgia Tech and his MBA with high distinction from Harvard University, where he was a Baker Scholar. He holds honorary PhDs from Georgia Institute of Technology, St. Thomas University, and Bryant University.

Bill and his wife, Penny, reside in Minneapolis and Boston. They have two sons: Jeff George, who lives in Munich, Germany, with his wife, Renee Will, and daughter, Dylan; and Jon George, MD, who lives in San Francisco with his wife, Jeannette Lager, MD, and son, Freeman.

Bill's Web site is billgeorge.org and his Twitter address is @bill_george.

DOUG BAKER

There have been five major arcs in Doug's life that weave together to give meaning to his involvement in the creation of this book.

The first arc, in the corporate world, began after he received his undergraduate degree from the University of Texas and his MBA from the Stanford Graduate School of Business. As a marketing manager at the Pillsbury Company, he was exposed to organizational and leadership development concepts that led him to adopt this work as his career focus.

After several years as Pillsbury's director of training, he began his second arc in joining a consulting firm, where he gained further proficiency in developing teams into highly effective groups. In parallel, his teaching arc began with positions at Gustavus Adolphus College and the University of St. Thomas (St. Paul).

His consulting practice led him to join a former client, Litton Microwave Cooking Products, where he served as vice president of human resources while Bill George was president. This was followed by another period of consulting with a wide range of organizations, including 3M, Control Data, Dain Bosworth, First Bank System, Honeywell, Investors Diversified Services, and the state of Minnesota. In all these assignments, emphasis was on improving organizational effectiveness through effective leaders working well together as teams.

The corporate arc surfaced for the last time when he joined American Express Financial Advisors (successor to Investors Diversified Services) as senior vice president of human resources. After twelve years, he returned to his practice of consulting, executive coaching, and mentoring. His consulting work focused on team and executive effectiveness. During this time he coauthored *Twelve-Step Wisdom at Work* and wrote articles for magazines and newspapers.

Concurrently, his teaching as an executive fellow in the University of St. Thomas Opus College of Business graduate program led to becoming a moderator of the Aspen Great Books Seminar. He cofounded the Legacy Center, which provides seminars and educational materials encouraging people to leave their stories, values, and acquired wisdom for their successors.

During the past decade, Doug has developed Conversations of Consequence, helping leaders in their communities to form groups using the True North Groups model. Now he is forming the True North Groups Institute to assist individuals and organizations developing these groups and to provide advice to existing groups.

A fourth arc has been service to the community as he has served on numerous educational, arts, business, and nonprofit boards.

The final arc is Doug's family, which consists of his wife, Carole; their son, Doug, Jr., his wife, Julie, and their three children; his daughter Julia McLean and her four children; and his daughter Susan Winkelmann, her husband, Ed, and their three daughters.

THE TRUE NORTH GROUPS INSTITUTE
Support for Your True North Group

ONE OF OUR GOALS IN WRITING THIS BOOK IS TO encourage widespread formation of True North Groups. To support you in this process, we have established the True North Groups Institute to provide assistance to organizations and individuals who want to form a True North Group or strengthen their existing group. Institute leaders are available to provide:

- Facilitation of the formation of new True North Groups among individuals and within organizations
- Customized True North Group installations
- Help-line support for existing groups wishing to improve their effectiveness
- Speakers for organizations and leaders on the use of True North groups as a leadership development practice
- A repository for stories of successful groups and the favorite memories of members
- A registry of professional facilitators to assist in new group formation
- A registry for people interested in joining a group that can be shared with similar people in nearby locations
- A source for books, articles, and materials to aid in group formation and effectiveness

To contact us, please refer to our Web site: truenorthgroupsinstitute.com

You may also contact us at: thetruenorthgroups@gmail.com

To contact Bill George about leadership opportunities, speeches, or seminars, please refer to his Web site, billgeorge.org, or e-mail him at online@bpgeorge.com.

Berrett–Koehler
BK Publishers

Berrett-Koehler is an independent publisher dedicated to an ambitious mission: *Creating a World That Works for All*.

We believe that to truly create a better world, action is needed at all levels—individual, organizational, and societal. At the individual level, our publications help people align their lives with their values and with their aspirations for a better world. At the organizational level, our publications promote progressive leadership and management practices, socially responsible approaches to business, and humane and effective organizations. At the societal level, our publications advance social and economic justice, shared prosperity, sustainability, and new solutions to national and global issues.

A major theme of our publications is "Opening Up New Space." Berrett-Koehler titles challenge conventional thinking, introduce new ideas, and foster positive change. Their common quest is changing the underlying beliefs, mindsets, institutions, and structures that keep generating the same cycles of problems, no matter who our leaders are or what improvement programs we adopt.

We strive to practice what we preach—to operate our publishing company in line with the ideas in our books. At the core of our approach is stewardship, which we define as a deep sense of responsibility to administer the company for the benefit of all of our "stakeholder" groups: authors, customers, employees, investors, service providers, and the communities and environment around us.

We are grateful to the thousands of readers, authors, and other friends of the company who consider themselves to be part of the "BK Community." We hope that you, too, will join us in our mission.

A BK Business Book

This book is part of our BK Business series. BK Business titles pioneer new and progressive leadership and management practices in all types of public, private, and nonprofit organizations. They promote socially responsible approaches to business, innovative organizational change methods, and more humane and effective organizations.

Berrett–Koehler
Publishers

A community dedicated to creating
a world that works for all

Visit Our Website: www.bkconnection.com

Read book excerpts, see author videos and Internet movies, read
our authors' blogs, join discussion groups, download book apps, find
out about the BK Affiliate Network, browse subject-area libraries of
books, get special discounts, and more!

Subscribe to Our Free E-Newsletter, the *BK Communiqué*

Be the first to hear about new publications, special discount offers,
exclusive articles, news about bestsellers, and more! Get on the list
for our free e-newsletter by going to **www.bkconnection.com**.

Get Quantity Discounts

Berrett-Koehler books are available at quantity discounts for orders
of ten or more copies. Please call us toll-free at (800) 929-2929 or
email us at bkp.orders@aidcvt.com.

Join the BK Community

BKcommunity.com is a virtual meeting place where people from
around the world can engage with kindred spirits to create a world
that works for all. **BKcommunity.com** members may create their own
profiles, blog, start and participate in forums and discussion groups,
post photos and videos, answer surveys, announce and register for
upcoming events, and chat with others online in real time. Please join
the conversation!